Cambridge Elements

Elements in England in the Early Medieval World
edited by
Megan Cavell
University of Birmingham
Rory Naismith
University of Cambridge
Winfried Rudolf
University of Göttingen
Emily V. Thornbury
Yale University

LITERARY FORM IN EARLY MEDIEVAL ENGLAND

Jennifer A. Lorden
William & Mary

CAMBRIDGE UNIVERSITY PRESS

Shaftesbury Road, Cambridge CB2 8EA, United Kingdom

One Liberty Plaza, 20th Floor, New York, NY 10006, USA

477 Williamstown Road, Port Melbourne, VIC 3207, Australia

314–321, 3rd Floor, Plot 3, Splendor Forum, Jasola District Centre, New Delhi – 110025, India

103 Penang Road, #05–06/07, Visioncrest Commercial, Singapore 238467

Cambridge University Press is part of Cambridge University Press & Assessment, a department of the University of Cambridge.

We share the University's mission to contribute to society through the pursuit of education, learning and research at the highest international levels of excellence.

www.cambridge.org
Information on this title: www.cambridge.org/9781009663281

DOI: 10.1017/9781009328630

© Jennifer A. Lorden 2025

This publication is in copyright. Subject to statutory exception and to the provisions of relevant collective licensing agreements, no reproduction of any part may take place without the written permission of Cambridge University Press & Assessment.

When citing this work, please include a reference to the DOI 10.1017/9781009328630

First published 2025

A catalogue record for this publication is available from the British Library

ISBN 978-1-009-66328-1 Hardback
ISBN 978-1-009-32861-6 Paperback
ISSN 2632-203X (online)
ISSN 2632-2021 (print)

Cambridge University Press & Assessment has no responsibility for the persistence or accuracy of URLs for external or third-party internet websites referred to in this publication and does not guarantee that any content on such websites is, or will remain, accurate or appropriate.

For EU product safety concerns, contact us at Calle de José Abascal, 56, 1°, 28003 Madrid, Spain, or email eugpsr@cambridge.org

Literary Form in Early Medieval England

Elements in England in the Early Medieval World

DOI: 10.1017/9781009328630
First published online: April 2025

Jennifer A. Lorden
William & Mary

Author for correspondence: Jennifer A. Lorden, jalorden@wm.edu

Abstract: The earliest English writers left little comment on their literary forms. In contrast to the grammatical treatises of late antiquity or critical studies of contemporary and modern literature, early medieval English writing offers only sparse contemporaneous self-commentary, often in brief or conventional notes along the way to other things. But Old English and Latin literature had lively and evolving practices of literary form and formal innovation. *Literary Form in Early Medieval England* examines both more and lesser known forms, considering the multilingual landscape of early medieval England and showing that Old English literary forms do not simply end with the rupture of the Norman Conquest but continue in surprising ways. *Literary Form in Early Medieval England* offers a concise tour of what we do know of literary forms, both those that have received more attention and those that have been relatively overlooked, across the first six centuries of English literature.

Keywords: early medieval England, Old English, Anglo-Latin, Early Middle English, literary form

© Jennifer A. Lorden 2025

ISBNs: 9781009663281 (HB), 9781009328616 (PB), 9781009328630 (OC)
ISSNs: 2632-203X (online), 2632-2021 (print)

Contents

Introduction	1
1 Verse Forms	7
2 Mixed Forms: Prose and Verse	19
3 Prose Forms	29
4 Plain and Standard Styles	41
5 Later Forms	49
Afterword: What Is Form For?	59
Bibliography	63

Introduction

Early English writers left little surviving comment about literary form. Where late antique writers left grammatical and rhetorical treatises and modern authors offer interviews and craft workshops, early medieval English literature, from between roughly 500 and 1100 CE, exists now with only sparse contemporaneous self-commentary. In the rare extant cases when writers of this early period do speak about their own writing, they do so often in brief and sometimes conventional notes along the way to other things – in a prologue to a story, or a comment on a translation. But a lack of surviving commentary does not entail a lack of conscious, deliberate thought about literary form, and we can know little of what orally transmitted knowledge has been lost to later centuries. Literary forms bear meaning through shared cultural understandings, through use and reuse in different literary contexts. These shared understandings often express most powerfully what they do not need to comment on explicitly, because the expectation of understanding becomes part of what they have to say. In spite of these silences that, centuries later, confront modern readers who seek to understand these early texts, literary form and formal innovation were lively and evolving across both of the major literary languages of this earliest period, Old English and Latin. This Element considers how the literary forms of early medieval England may be understood, why they matter to modern readers, and how they take their place in broader and longer literary histories. It seeks to offer a concise tour of what we do know of early medieval English literary forms, both those that have received more attention and those that have been relatively overlooked from across the first six centuries of English literature.

In modern understanding of this period of English literature, a fairly small number of often-anthologized texts, mainly in vernacular verse, predominate academic and popular understanding of the period – including *Beowulf*, a poem adapted into films and comics and novel adaptations. Beyond this, poems such as the Old English elegies (notably *The Wanderer* or *The Seafarer*), or perhaps *The Dream of the Rood*, are anthologized enough to be somewhat familiar to nonspecialists. But literary form in in the period was not limited to literary texts considered canonical in a later age, nor to only poetic texts, much less to poetic texts only in English rather than Latin. These better-remembered texts are best understood as part of a much more complex, broad literary landscape. This Element, then, sets these better-known texts alongside texts and forms from the period that modern readers might have encountered less often, including examples of prose and plain style that have at times attracted less critical attention. To do so, this Element will tour the multilingual landscape of early medieval England and show that Old English literary forms do not simply end with the rupture of the Norman Conquest but continue in surprising ways. This Element moves through various contingent categories of early literary forms in England, proceeding broadly from the more to less obviously formally complex, from the formally intricate to the apparently "unmarked" forms of literary prose. Each variety of form raises questions about its literary and cultural functions.

The literature of early medieval England may be considered to encompass the time from the conversion, at the turn of the seventh century, of the Angles, Saxons, and Jutes who had arrived from the European continent and settled in Britain in the fifth and sixth centuries, until the period just following the Norman Conquest in 1066, when the English language and English literary forms began to change rapidly. The history of literature in early medieval England begins with the arrival of the people groups who would become the English, and who spoke the Germanic dialects that would become the various forms of the Old English language. Apart from some runic inscriptions, the literary language of those peoples, as it survives, begins with their conversion to Christianity beginning around the turn of the seventh century BCE. The conversion and the cultural changes that followed necessitated and enabled substantial bodies of writing as Christian teachers instituted literate religious instruction. Literacy began to flourish in the early schools of Augustine of Canterbury, further developed by the Syrian Theodore and North African Hadrian in the seventh century.[1] They not only established institutions for teaching English clergy to read in Latin and Greek but also brought with them texts and textual traditions that would shape the earliest literary traditions among the English. For one, the form of the *enigmata*, or riddle collection, extends from the Latin North African writer Symphosius, through a collection from Theodore and Hadrian's student Aldhelm of Malmesbury, and carries on in collections by English writers Eusebius, Tatwine, and Boniface, and finally in the vernacular, in the Old English Exeter riddles that contain riddles adapted from Symphosius himself. From these beginnings, Old English literature becomes a uniquely early body of vernacular literature in Europe, producing poetry, homilies, translations, and legal texts in English alongside Latin.

At the latter end of the early English period, after the Norman Conquest of 1066, French takes the place of English alongside Latin as the dominant languages of the ruling class and of the church. The aftermath of the Norman Conquest supplanted English institutions and literary traditions, as well as many of the venues in which English itself had been used. But English texts nevertheless continue to be written while other texts continued to be translated into

---

[1] Lapidge, "School of Theodore and Hadrian."

English, as the vernacular of the people and thus an indispensable language for preaching and teaching English laypersons in the language they could best understand, and a literary tradition for their teachers to draw upon.[2]

Insular literature was never so insulated as accounts of its history have sometimes been. To take up one example, Alcuin and the missionaries led by Boniface brought English learning and English textual forms to the continent in the eighth century. Or for another, the Benedictine Reforms brought continental learning into English monastic institutions in the tenth. And English literature translated from Latin sources evinces evolving and at least partial knowledge of the broader world of the Mediterranean, of West and South Asia, and of Northern Africa. From these varied, multilingual sources, early medieval England developed and adapted the varieties of forms used throughout the period: both poetic and prose forms and combinations thereof, in both Old English and Latin, and with styles of writing and syntax at times arcane and highly ornamented, at times deceptively simple.

The earliest modern scholars of this period, however, largely came to Old English and the study of early medieval England through Germanic philology in the eighteenth and nineteenth centuries. Their interest in uncovering the cultures of the early peoples who spoke the mutually intelligible languages of Old English, Old Norse, Old Saxon, Old High German, and related languages laid crucial ground work for understanding surviving texts in these languages. Yet these scholars also prioritized an interest in the primitive origins of modern nations and people groups including, when it came to medieval England, a pre-Christian, pagan past with little of the evidence those scholars might have hoped to find there.[3] The use of the hyphenated term "Anglo-Saxon" came into currency in the nineteenth century, collapsing into a single group the continental peoples who migrated into what would become England, and conceptualizing them as a national group in a way that they could not in the early part of the period have conceived of themselves.[4] Within this paradigm, poems like *Beowulf* or the *Battle of Maldon* – that is, poems imagined to reflect a lingering heroic-warrior ethos – were considered more central, and more centrally "English," than, for example, vernacular poems based on Latin lives of Mediterranean saints. Although most modern scholars would not consciously subscribe to the ideals of their nineteenth-century predecessors, the early emphasis and large body of work on these texts have shaped both popular

---

[2] Irvine, "Compilation and Use of Old English Manuscripts," 60–61; Watson, *Balaam's Ass*, 20–21, 147, 195–211.

[3] Stanley, *Search for Anglo-Saxon Paganism*; Niles, *Idea of Anglo-Saxon England*; and Rambaran-Olm, "A Wrinkle in Medieval Time," 390–91.

[4] Wilton, "What Do We Mean by *Anglo-Saxon*?"

conceptions of the period and the works that have continued to be most anthologized and studied. Even in scholarship, ideas of the period continue to be influenced by historiography dating back to the English Reformation, contrasting modern secular "enlightenment" with supposed medieval repression and superstition.[5] Within medieval studies, the early Middle Ages has served much the same purpose for narratives of the "high" and later Middle Ages, serving as a "primitive" backdrop for narratives of later progress and cultural achievement.[6]

The project of understanding the past can never be completed. For this reason, categorizing the past into periods and aspects of the past into specializations makes a certain practical academic sense – no scholar or even generation of scholars could hope to turn every stone along the path to reconstructing myriad past forms and the cultures that produced them. Yet inevitably, the dividing lines come to be drawn according to the interests and a priori assumptions of the peoples and times that draw them. As subsequent generations then build upon that foundational work, they may wittingly or not reproduce the assumptions, priorities, and prejudices of earlier moments in the history of the field. The tendency of scholars from the nineteenth century to the present to seek the histories of modern nations in the Middle Ages, for example, led scholars' conceptions of cultural groups to coalesce broadly around national identities that did not yet exist in the Middle Ages.[7] Meanwhile, for the study of literary history in particular, the formation of academic language departments around modern languages (such as English, French, German, or Italian) has similarly prioritized literary histories as studied through the lens of modern nations, often those that have spoken and imposed European languages through colonization. These historical and institutional dynamics have the effect of diminishing academic attention to multilingual, multicultural exchange among medieval peoples. Latinate literary culture, for example, which linked peoples across Christian Europe, the Mediterranean, and Northern Africa, remains important to medievalists – who nevertheless usually work in language departments focused on adjacent vernaculars. For these reasons, scholars have called those boundaries of period and subfield into question.[8] Interrogating and reframing approaches to the field can bring scholars of older periods into conversation with contemporary ideas, but it can also allow the field to work more comprehensively and indeed more rigorously on questions that had

---

[5] Davis, *Periodization and Sovereignty*, 3–4; Watson, *Balaam's Ass*, 15, 89–90.
[6] Rambaran-Olm, "A Wrinkle in Medieval Time," 387.
[7] Reynolds, "What Do We Mean by 'Anglo-Saxon' and 'Anglo-Saxons'?" esp. 396–401; Wilton, "What Do We Mean by *Anglo-Saxon*?" 425–56.
[8] Davis, *Periodization and Sovereignty*, 6–7; Rambaran-Olm, "A Wrinkle in Medieval Time"; Treharne, "Categorization, Periodization," 247–48.

been overlooked by previous generations, to apply ongoing questions to texts that have rarely been studied, to uncover historical phenomena and values that we had not been expected to find. Studying the past can also oblige us to study the history of that study, broadening and sharpening our focus by turns to see what has been omitted from the frame or overlooked in broad landscapes.

Working from the premise that critical understanding of the past must complicate the very boundaries it creates, I divide the earliest literature from England into broad categories *precisely* to work against those categories, as the forms of literary texts in the wild boisterously sprawl across them. Poetry, prose (including glosses), and mixed forms that juxtapose verse and prose together, in both Old English and Latin, offer rough conceptual starting points that immediately reveal the interconnectedness of the literary forms the texts that contain them actually use. That interconnectedness is, of course, germane to all literature, which generally refuses the categorical boundaries we use to talk about it. But early English forms have distinctive connections across texts and genres, exhibit particular formal habits of allusion, and work themselves out in different ways in the works of different writers across the period. These forms are best understood in relation to one another, because they were in conversation with one another in the period in which they were produced. The few examples of critical and metacritical commentary on form that do survive from early England, in texts such as Bede's *De schematibus et tropis* or the versions of the Old English *Boethius*, in glosses or comments in texts themselves, offer clues to how early medieval writers thought about the functions of the literary forms they used while embodying literary forms in and of themselves. Formal and generic categories are not the only ones that the present survey calls into question. Early medieval English writers learned, first, from teachers from beyond English shores, and continued to exchange knowledge with thinkers on the continent, both through English writers who worked abroad or through foreign figures who came to England. Norse skalds, for example, were active in the courts of English kings.[9] And while the Norman Conquest brought about the permanent ruptures that would rapidly shift the English language and introduce new influences upon literature in England, English continued and its forms evolved into new animals rather than going entirely extinct. In other words, to understand the literary forms of early medieval England, we have to look beyond the boundaries of form and beyond England and the "early" medieval period entirely, crossing both the geographical and historical boundaries that would eventually be drawn around them.

---

[9] Frank, "A Taste for Knottiness," 197–200.

The first part of this Element begins with verse forms, and the conventions and structures that define verse in early England in both English and Latin. Considering verse requires considering the more-anthologized texts alongside lesser-appreciated didactic poems or macaronic verse or poems adapted from other sources, as well as considering the stakes of ongoing metrical debates for broader literary histories. This section necessarily leads into the second, on "mixed forms," or texts that formally combine or juxtapose verse and prose. These forms both complicate and require distinctions between verse and prose forms, as texts move playfully between them. This section considers both prosimetrical texts, that is, texts that alternate between prose and verse sections, as well as the form of the *opus geminatum*, or twinned work, in which authors present similar content in both verse and prose versions, often designed to be read together. Section 3, then, considers the complexity of prose forms. Although prose might naturally seem to be the form best suited to simply conveying information, prose in both Latin and Old English in the early period nonetheless exhibits complex formal features, from stylized alliterating language to conventional narrative structures like prologues that help situate an audience culturally conditioned to understand them. A further section on "plain and standard styles" cuts across these generic categories, considering the ways that early medieval English writers both employed plain style or, at least, rhetorically valorized a plain manner of speaking. Distinct from this are standard vocabularies and dialects, from the "Standard Old English" that uses a West Saxon dialect for literary texts across regions, or the "Winchester Vocabulary" that sought to standardize vocabulary in contexts connected to the institutions of the Benedictine Reform. All of these sections, too, consider the issues of translation as literary forms are retained, altered, or remade across new versions of texts. Finally, Section 5 considers the late style of early medieval England, and the forms of literature immediately following the Norman Conquest. As French-speaking Normans came to dominate political and ecclesiastical institutions, Anglo-Norman French took up its place as an English vernacular alongside Latin as a language of both government and the church. But English persisted, as a language of pastoral care and as a language copied and annotated for centuries to come. Although the preservation of Old English largely peters out around the end of the twelfth century, conventions of the vernacular tradition continue in early Middle English works that combine those conventions with those introduced in the new literary milieu of post-Conquest England.

Across the Element as a whole, the permeability of literary forms comes to the fore – indeed part of the creation of literary form in the medieval period relies on the use of, for example, homiletic conventions in poetry and vice versa, and an audience's recognition of forms from literary works that had come before. Nowhere is this more apparent than in the formulaicity of Old English poetry, whereby poetic half-lines can be used and reused in different verse contexts, or the use of narrative conceits across both homily and verse, for example. Early medieval English forms operate in part by being recognizable across texts – their apparently staid facade belied by the webs of associations evoked by a formulaic phrase, a type scene, an allusion, or a homiletic injunction.[10] Only by attending carefully to these forms within as much of this broader cultural web of meaning as possible can we hope to begin reconstructing how they operated for their earliest audiences.

Considering early medieval forms requires close reading, and inevitably many more relevant sources exist than can be closely analyzed and juxtaposed in a volume of this length. There remains, too, much that we do not know about the contexts that produced specific early medieval texts as they survive to us. But thinking about form requires that we look beyond the forms themselves as well, to understand how early medieval writers understood, used, and talked about their forms, and also how modern readers have understood or endeavored to understand them. Thinking about early forms requires us to think across the customary boundary of the Norman Conquest, to consider the stakes of defining early forms as such, and to think about what inheritance they might have left to the literary forms that followed them.

Particular forms and formal literary texts have been prioritized in modern scholarship. Yet the array of forms and formal approaches in early medieval English literature, and their shifts across time, make the case that readers now can only understand early literary culture in England by considering the full array of the play of forms in early medieval England, across the languages in which those forms were written.

1 Verse Forms

Early medieval England was home to two major verse traditions, in Old English and Latin, and neighbor to others, in Welsh, Irish, Old Norse, and Old Saxon, among others. These traditions had distinctive formal conventions as well as correspondences as they interacted over time. One of the central descriptors of Old English poetic form is one that would sound insulting if applied to modern poetry: Old English poetry is formulaic, repetitive, and each poem relies heavily on the connotations established by a broader body of Old English poetry already in existence. Old English poems are almost always anonymous, and the very conventionality and self-referentiality of Old English poetry becomes its defining feature, depending on allusions and associations implanted from repetition in other

---

[10] See, for example, Foley, *Immanent Art*; Lorden, *Forms of Devotion*, 5–7.

contexts, and revealing new ways of reusing formulaic elements in new contexts to create new effects resonant with the old. Early English poets write in Latin as well as the vernacular, and although Anglo-Latin poems continue to be disproportionately understudied, we often know things about them that we often do not know about their Old English counterparts, from the names of their authors to the purported occasion and motivation of their composition. Early English poets write in forms of Latin that echo and depart from those of other continental poets and one another. And in Latin, unlike Old English, early medieval English poets do leave explanatory comment both on the workings of Latin meter as they understood it and on the kinds of Latin meter they preferred. These Anglo-Latin poetic forms also interact with early English ones, creating a complex landscape of poetic form across the first centuries of literary history in England. Although we often lack comment from early medieval English writers on their own forms, and although we may often lack information on the date or location of a composition, to say nothing of information about a poem's author, we can nonetheless learn much about the earliest English verse forms from the ways that those forms engage in conversation with *other* forms. In beginning with a reconsideration of the most widely known literary forms, this section will make a case for greater attention to those forms often overlooked in standard scholarly accounts of the earliest English poetry.

The basic structure of Old English verse comprises long lines each composed of two half lines, as we see at the beginning of Cædmon's Hymn:

> Nu sculon herigean   heofonrices Weard
> meotodes meahte   and his modgeþanc.[11]
>
> [Now let us praise the Guardian of the heavenly kingdom,
> the Measurer's might and the plans of his mind]

The standard half line features two stressed syllables; the stressed syllables in the first half may alliterate with each other and at least one of these alliterates with *only* one of the two stressed syllables in the second half, as in "**M**eotodes **m**eahte | and his **m**odgeþanc" in the quoted example. In modern editions, two half-lines are set in a single line, with a space between the half-lines indicating the dividing line between them, often called a "caesura." But if one were to look at a page in an Old English poetic manuscript, the lines and half-lines are written straight across the page, without line breaks and with inconsistent spacing even between words and syllables. What modern editions represent through line breaks and punctuation seems to have been intuitively recognized by the poetry's original readers.[12]

---

[11] Krapp and Dobbie, eds., *Anglo-Saxon Poetic Records*, vol. VI, 105–6.
[12] O'Brien O'Keeffe, *Visible Song*, 3–8.

Nearly every other aspect of Old English meter continues to be a topic of debate, and there are both exceptions to the rules above and further rules that have proved more challenging for scholars to define. Old English writers left no surviving metrical treatises analogous to the *Skáldskaparmál* and *Háttatal* in Snorri's *Prose Edda* in Old Norse. The most influential early systemization of Old English meter was that of Eduard Sievers, who identified "five types" of possible Old English poetic half lines based on their patterns of stressed and unstressed syllables.[13] Many revisions and competing theories have arisen to further refine our understanding of the metrical model in the decades since, from arguments that Old English poetry does not distinguish between verse and prose at all,[14] to foundational work seeking to ascertain the relative dating of Old English poems based on metrical changes,[15] to recognizing metrical position and prosody as more determinative than syllable stress.[16] Perhaps most importantly, metrists have demonstrated that vernacular alliterative meter does not die out after the Norman Conquest, only to be resurrected in an "alliterative revival" during the later Middle English period, but evolves as the English language does, remaining the dominant metrical form for half a dozen centuries and more.[17]

Old English poetry famously only has one type of meter, the alliterative long line, although scholars continue to debate just how this basic poetic meter worked, and there are exceptions to the rule. So-called hypermetric verses are common enough to complicate matters, and a few poems contain lines or refrains that seem to play by rules of their own. Moreover, there is, of course, much more to poetic form than meter. Longer poetic texts, from poems like *Beowulf* to *Exodus* to verse saints' lives, may be structured with prologues or hortatory conclusions. Homiletic language interweaves with poetic formulae in devotional poems. Some poems, such as the verse *Solomon and Saturn*, take the form of verse dialogues, and some poems (like *Deor*, or *Wulf and Eadwacer*) use refrains or repetition. Shorter poems in Old English, such as many of the elegiac poems most anthologized and widely taught aside from *Beowulf*, are hardly seen at all outside of the single manuscript known as the Exeter Book. And since poetry was written in Latin as well as in English, both languages interact within poems and within manuscripts containing poetry. While Anglo-Latin verse

---

[13] Sievers, *Altgermanische Metrik*. [14] Beechy, *The Poetics of Old English*.
[15] Fulk, *History of Old English Meter*.
[16] Yakovlev, "Development of Alliterative Metre"; Cornelius and Weiskott, "Intricacies of Counting to Four"; as well as Cornelius, *Reconstructing Alliterative Verse*, 7–8; and Weiskott, *English Alliterative Verse*.
[17] See Hanna, "Alliterative Poetry"; Weiskott, *English Alliterative Verse*; Cornelius, *Reconstructing Alliterative Verse*.

often replicated classical meters, poets like Aldhelm and Alcuin also blended alliterative patterns reminiscent of vernacular poetry into Latin metrical forms.

But more than its single consistent metrical pattern, Old English vernacular verse also repeats, with or without variation, entire half lines within poems and between poems, as well as tropes and poetic "type scenes."[18] Each of these units, from the smallest half line to the most elaborate narrative scene, does more than reuse available poetic material: it brings with it the literary associations of other uses of that formula or scene, subtly shading the connotations of the verse in its new context. To take one example, the formulaic half line "þæt was ___ cyning" (that was a ___ king) appears several times in the poem *Beowulf*.[19] In the poem's opening lines, the formulaic phrase "þæt wæs god cyning" (that was a good king, *Beowulf* 11b) straightforwardly asserts the qualities of Scyld Scefing that made him a great ruler: establishing bonds of loyalty among his people through generosity and dominance over his enemies through military might. By the time the phrase appears again, it appears to deny that King Hrothgar should bear blame for his inability to protect his people from Grendel, prefaced by a careful "but": "ac þæt wæs god cyning" (but that was a good king; 862b). The phrase appears again, much later, to describe Beowulf as a "god cyning" – just in time for him to die fighting a dragon and leave his people defenseless (2390b). As John Miles Foley has argued, these formulaic phrases accumulate meaning through their repeated uses, bringing the previous connotations of the phrase into their new contexts.[20] In the poem *Deor*, the poet can remark of Eormanric, "þæt wæs **grim** cyning" (that was a **cruel** king; 23b) and the condemnation of this reversal of the formula echoes discordantly with all the good kings that have gone before.[21] Clusters of formulaic phrases coincide between *Beowulf* and the Old English poem *Andreas*, suggesting not just the poems' reliance on the earlier verse tradition but their ongoing, critical engagement with it.[22]

Beyond the use of formulaic phrases, Old English poetry also makes use of entire poetic "type scenes," often also including formulaic phrasing or verbal motifs, recalling the entire atmosphere of previously encountered poetic situations and dropping new characters and complexities into them. Such type scenes might include the trope of the "beasts of battle" or the "cliffs of death," or of an imposing figure's approach to a hall.[23] So, for example, several of the borrowed clusters of half lines in *Andreas* do not merely cluster but arrange the half lines in the same order as they appear in *Beowulf*,[24] suggesting

---

[18] Fry, "Old English Formulaic Themes and Type-Scenes."
[19] Quotations from Fulk, et al., eds., *Klaeber's* Beowulf.   [20] Foley, *Immanent Art*, 7.
[21] "Malone, ed., *Deor*."   [22] Friesen, "Visions and Revisions"; Powell, "Verbal Parallels."
[23] Fry, "Old English Formulaic Themes and Type-Scenes," 48–54.
[24] Friesen, "Visions and Revisions."

the *Andreas* poet wanted to recall not just the tradition in general but those episodes from *Beowulf* specifically, allowing their atmosphere and thematic parallels to shape and complicate the scene in *Andreas*.[25] These highly conventional elements contribute both to what Elizabeth Tyler has called a "poetics of the familiar," in which Old English poets play upon an audience's recognition of poetic elements from verse they have encountered before, and to what Renée Trilling has called an "aesthetics of nostalgia," whereby the archaic and often unchanging topoi, formulas, and scenes of Old English poetry collectively form a "constellation" of an imagined poetic past.[26] While focusing on very different aspects of Old English verse, these studies ask us to consider the role not so much of an individual author but of a communal tradition in the composition of Old English verse: "tradition is located not in a poet alone, but in a wider community."[27] This sense of a poetic community, that must recognize and judge poetic compositions, shaped the ways that early English poets approached their work, as Emily Thornbury has shown, whether those communities were clear and present ones or largely the imagined poetic communities found in books.[28] Poetic form can thus also tell us the histories of its making, even when we lack the information to locate an individual poem or its anonymous author in a specific place or time.

The opening lines of *Beowulf* evince many distinctively Old English formal features simultaneously:

> Hwæt, we Gar-Dena   in geardagum,
> Þeodcyninga   þrym gefrunon,
> hu ða æþelingas   ellen fremedon.
> Oft Scyld Scefing   sceaþena þreatum,
> monegum mægþum   meodosetla ofteah,
> egsode eorlas,   syððan ærest wearð
> feasceaft funden.   He þæs frofre gebad
> weox under wolcnum,   weorðmyndum þah,
> oðþæt him æghwylc   þara ymbsittendra
> ofer hronrade   hyran scolde,
> gomban gyldan.   Þæt wæs god cyning.[29]

[What! We have heard of the spear-Danes in the old days, of the people's kings, how the princes performed glory. Often Scyld Scefing with troops of warriors overthrew the mead benches of many peoples, terrified the noblemen, after he was first found destitute. He awaited consolation for that, grew

---

[25] Dumitrescu, *Experience of Education*, 104–25; Thomas, "A Close Fitt."
[26] Tyler, *Old English Poetics*, 2–4; Trilling, *Aesthetics of Nostalgia*.
[27] Tyler, *Old English Poetics*, 4.   [28] Thornbury, *Becoming a Poet*.
[29] Fulk, et al., eds., *Klaeber's* Beowulf, lines 1–11.

under the heavens, prospered in honor, until each of the surrounding peoples over the whale road should obey him, pay him tribute. That was a good king.]

This prologue follows a conventional form, identified by Eric Weiskott as one of the four types of conventional prologues that begin all long Old English poems.[30] Opening in the first-person plural, the poet calls upon a collective, shared knowledge, reminding the audience that this is something "we have heard" – at least rhetorically, the contents of the verses that follow are not meant to be original, but familiar to poet and audience alike, a recollection of and dream of a greater past now lost and in some sense unreachable except through songs like this one. And what does the glory of kings consist of? In part, the king's ability to gain treasure, specifically a treasure not to be hoarded, although covetable, but shared with his people to reinforce the bonds of loyalty between them. Here we find the aforementioned formulaic half-line "þæt wæs god cyning" (that was a good king); the triumphant example here becomes the metric by which to consider the other instances of this formula throughout the poem. Prologues like these invite variation upon familiar forms, but crucially ground their variety in familiarity – the audience may have heard this story before, but even if they had not, the prologue tells them what kind of a story this one is going to be.

Shared knowledge also underlies the aggressive allusiveness of Old English poems, which often tell stories by way of examples only partially related. The poems most studied, anthologized, and translated are *Beowulf* and the poems known as the "elegies," a term that, when it comes to Old English, refers to poems that are not so much a lament for a particular death as for the transience and inevitability of the death of all things in the world. But the shared stock of formulas that characterize these so-called elegiac poems appear in devotional verse, too, and indeed little of what survives of Old English poetry could be considered meaningfully secular in the modern sense. The Old English *Fates of the Apostles* opens with a similar "We have heard" prologue to *Beowulf*, and what the poem tells us about the apostles would not be quite enough to grasp their significance had we *not* heard their stories before. The poem *Deor* likewise presents its events so allusively that scholars had for decades assumed its episodes were unrelated, episodes better known to the poem's medieval audience than to modern scholars who might try to read it. It seems, however, that the allusions in the poem evoke a linear narrative sequence of related legendary events surrounding the family and associates of Weland the smith, but an audience would have to know the story already to be able to discern its full

[30] Weiskott, *English Alliterative Verse*.

significance in *Deor*'s elliptical verses.[31] A verse like "Ðeodric ahte þritig wintra/ Mæringa burg; þæt wæs monegum cuþ" (Theodric ruled the city of the Mærings for thirty winters; that was known to many) gives little context or even tonal cues for how we should understand Theodric or his rule – was it good or bad, or was its eventual end good or bad?[32] And in the Old English version, the stories Deor the poet relates lead him to a meditation on transience in the world and how that transience gestures toward God as the one abiding authority under whom all worldly turns of fortune are governed. Apart from *Deor*, fuller versions of the story of Weland and his son and the kings who determine their fortunes are told in the fragments of the Old English *Waldere*, and in *Volundarkviða* in the poetic Edda, and in *Þidreks saga* – and although the Norse texts necessarily only survive from after the Icelandic conversion to Christianity in the eleventh century and the subsequent advent of these texts' appearance in written form, the details among the texts remain consistent enough to attest to a shared stock of literary touchstones, a common knowledge of a legendary world. The story of *Deor*, and the allusive way in which the poem relates it, points to the larger difficulties modern readers have in recovering the shared, assumed cultural knowledge that Old English poems in particular exhibit, and the ways that scholarly priorities and assumptions have shaped and at times misdirected our efforts to recover that knowledge.

Modern readers encounter verse primarily as text on a page, but we know less about the ways that Old English poetry was experienced. Scholars had considered Old English poetry as an oral art form, following the influential work of Francis Magoun in 1953, based on Milman Parry and Albert Bates Lord's studies of Homer on the one hand, and of "unlettered" singers in twentieth-century Yugoslavia on the other.[33] But as Roberta Frank has demonstrated, our most vivid ideas of the oral poet, or *scop*, in pre-Conquest England are derived from the two or three fictive depictions in Old English poems featuring oral poets as characters, and these poems are all overt historical fictions – that is to say, not at all representations of the place and time that actually produced the poems we have, but *that* time's imagination of a distant past, long ago and far away.[34] In *Deor*, for example, the speaker describes having been the poet of the Heodenings, a legendary pre-Christian Scandinavian people whose entanglement in perpetual battle said to last until Ragnarok is related in various legends in Old Norse – nowhere near the time or place that the poem was recorded in

---

[31] Lorden, "Revisiting the Legendary History of *Deor*"; see also Brljak, "Unediting *Deor*."
[32] Malone, ed., *Deor*, lines 18–19.
[33] Magoun, "Oral-Formulaic Character of Anglo-Saxon Narrative Poetry," 446; see discussion in Foley, "Texts that Speak to Readers Who Hear," 142–44.
[34] Frank, "The Search for the Anglo-Saxon Oral Poet," 11–36.

tenth-century England.[35] Or, the scop in *Beowulf* sings in the hall of the hero's fortunes – also in a poem set in a legendary past in pagan Scandinavia, generally before the people who would become the English had even settled in Britain. And so one difficulty with studying the historical orality of Old English poetry is that oral performance, by its very nature, leaves no trace in the historical record; all the evidence we have of Old English poetry must be written down.

Moreover, we have artifacts from early medieval England that attest to the literate experience of written poetry, whatever auditory poetic experience might have coexisted with or preceded them. The signature passages of Cynewulf, for one, record the name of their ostensible author in runic characters that each represent a word when read aloud, but spell a name when viewed among the otherwise Latin letters in the manuscript: The name can only be discerned by a literate audience who sees the runes on the page. And artifacts like the Ruthwell Cross, with its runic verses engraved around images of the crucifixion, attest to the physical, visible experience of a literary text, even if some who saw the verses might not have been able to read them. All of the evidence for vernacular poetry that survives to us is textual evidence. Yet in seeking to discern the traces of an oral poetic past, scholarship nevertheless encourages us to consider the *aural* conventions and qualities of an Old English verse that, in the forms in which it survives to us, was already a literate poetry even as it relied on its audience's understandings of metrical patterns not visibly represented on the page.[36]

Of course, the majority of poetry written in early England was written not in English but in Latin, and Anglo-Latin verse even provides us with a handful of named poets who can be located in history. Anglo-Latin verse also, unlike Old English, tended to be written with line breaks in manuscripts, suggesting its status as a learned language, both in the sense of belonging to more educated, usually clerical audiences, but also in the sense of being a language that had to be learned, one not mutually intelligible with the vernacular. The presence of these line breaks also makes possible visual features like acrostics and chiasmus, and Anglo-Latin poets, following the models of late Latin poets like Venantius Fortunatus, made use of elaborate acrostics and "shaped" poems that provided both a textual and a visual experience to their literate readers.

The earliest Latinate poets in England were shaped by literary traditions from outside English shores, and their verse continued to shape the distinctive forms of Anglo-Latin poetry. As discussed in the previous section, in the decades after Augustine of Canterbury first undertook the conversion of the English to

---

[35] Malone, ed., *Deor*, 16.
[36] See O'Brien O'Keeffe, *Visible Song*; Donoghue, *How the Anglo-Saxons Read*.

Christianity in 597 CE, teachers were needed to instruct the English in the faith. Christianity is a religion of the book, and the book for medieval Christians was the Latin Vulgate translation of the Bible; the nascent English church thus needed to be instructed in Latin. Theodore of Tarsus, in what is now Syria, and the abbot Hadrian, from northern Africa, were the two most influential teachers whose influence remains known to us. The Latin written by the early English Christians was deliberately complex; as Michael Lapidge has written, their Latin was characterized by "lavish display of vocabulary designed to impress by the arcane nature of its learning; it abounds in obscure, learned-sounding words, such as archaisms, grecisms, and neologisms."[37] This Latin style came to be known as hermeneutic Latin, after the *hermeneumata*, the glossaries from which they derived their vocabulary. At least one scholar has argued that the Latin written by the early English who learned from these early missionaries and teachers bears formal features similar to those of North African Latin, as the English were, in fact, directly taught Latin by North Africans.[38] Early medieval English writers thus develop a Latin with sometimes complex syntax, neologisms, and loan words distinct from those used on the European continent.

Beyond this traceable history of Latinate literary forms in general, we know more about early English thinking about poetic form in Latin in particular from the authors themselves. As little as the early English had to say about the forms of their vernacular poetry, they had as much to say about the forms of Latin verse, both in its basic technical requirements and in the stylistic flourishes that they themselves preferred. Aldhelm composed both the *De metris* and *De pedem regulis*, and ostensibly offered his *Enigmata* or riddle-poems (all one hundred of them) to demonstrate the form of the Latin hexameter. But he also seems to have developed a form of his own, a rhythmical meter of continuous octosyllables, that would come to be used for Latin verse by generations of English poets to come.[39] As one of the early poets to compose Latin meter who was not a native speaker of Latin, and one purportedly with less intuitive sense of subtleties of metrical variation, Aldhelm displays a greater tendency than classical poets to write in end-stopped lines, and a lesser tendency to make use of elision. But he does display an intriguing use of alliteration, far in excess of what classical Latin poets would have, and poetic formulae, suggesting the influence of vernacular English poetry on Aldhelm's Latin verse.[40] To whatever extent these tendencies may have suggested Aldhelm's approaching Latin poetry from an English vernacular tradition, they would become, in later

---

[37] Lapidge, *Anglo-Latin Literature*, I, 4–5.   [38] Carlson, "Africa and England," 12–32.
[39] Lapidge, *Anglo-Latin Literature*, I, 7–8.   [40] Lapidge, *Anglo-Latin Literature*, I, 255–57.

centuries, hallmarks of Anglo-Latin poetic forms, including deliberate use of Aldhelmian poetic phrases in collections structured upon Aldhelmian models.[41]

In the generation following Aldhelm, Bede, the venerable monk of Wearmouth-Jarrow, composed Latin poetry on devotional and hagiographic subjects, and wrote influential treatises on Latin meter and rhetorical forms. He demonstrated his skill as both a student and a teacher of Latin verse, putting into practice the same methods that he explores in his metrical treatises. In his *De arte metrica*, he sets out the forms of Latin poetry that he prefers – grouping noun and adjective pairs around finite verbs, making extensive use of enjambment – that he would also use in his own verse.[42] Alongside the *De arte metrica*, Bede also offers the *De schematibus et tropis*, setting out the variety of rhetorical figures that poets might also put to use. As Michael Lapidge has argued, Bede's Latin poetry, historically dismissed as merely technically proficient, continues a formal tradition of what Bede explicitly named as "the best kind of dactylic verse."[43] Valuing features like enjambment and asyndeton, Bede himself strove to exhibit those features in poems like his *Vita metrica Sancti Cuthberti* and his *De die judicii*. Bede wrote most of his poetry in hexameters, but also wrote hymns in lyric meters and poetry in elegiac couplets, including his hymn to St. Æthelthryth in his *Historia ecclesiastica*. Across these meters, Bede makes prominent use of internal rhyme, deploying rhyming syllables before the medial caesura and at the end of a line of verse.[44]

After the early flourishing of the school of Theodore and Hadrian, and writers and poets like Aldhelm and Bede who arose in the generations that followed, Anglo-Latin poetry traveled to the continent, where Alcuin of York composed in conversation with other Carolingian writers, training a new generation of Latin poets including Hrabanus Maurus. English Latin verse at this time continued to display a distinctively English poetic accent, importing features like alliteration and unusual vocabulary full of neologisms. If Alcuin's Carolingian-influenced poetry declined some of the use of neologisms and archaic, Greek-inspired vocabulary, he nevertheless retained features such as alliteration that had defined Anglo-Latin poets in the generations before him.[45] As English culture in turn reflected continental influence through the Benedictine Reforms of the tenth century, we see the continuing interactions of continental and English literary culture. After Lantfred of Fleury comes to Winchester from the continent to compose a hagiography of the English St. Swithun, the English Wulfstan Cantor composes a versified version of Lantfred's life in Latin, adding his own

---

[41] Clark, "Familiar Distances," 41–50.   [42] Lapidge, ed. and trans., *Bede's Latin Poetry*, 3.
[43] Lapidge, ed. and trans., *Bede's Latin Poetry*, 3.
[44] Lapidge, ed. and trans., *Bede's Latin Poetry*, 26.
[45] Bullough, "Reminiscence and Reality," 180.

Literary Form in Early Medieval England 17

flourishes as a Winchester local. The monastic Latin of this era represents what has been called Hermeneutic Latin, the form of Anglo-Latin requiring a high level of facility with Latin grammar and familiarity with its arcane vocabulary – that is, Latin distinct from that of the Carolingians, for instance, where Latin would have been mutually intelligible with the Romance-language vernacular.[46] The extreme example of Hermeneutic Latin verse might be a poem like the *Breviloquum Vitae Wilfridi* of Frithegod (like Lantfred, a writer educated in Francia), a verse retelling of the life of St. Wilfrid so dense and with vocabulary so arcane that it resists understanding even for readers with an account of the life handy for comparison.[47]

Translation of various kinds becomes another mode of interaction between Latinate and vernacular forms of English verse. Bede's *De die judicii* appears in another form in Old English verse, showing how the conventional forms of Latin poetry were adapted into and in conversation with vernacular forms. Indeed, Old English poems like *The Phoenix* or *Aldhelm* feature macaronic verses, switching between Old English and Latin in the middle of each long line, showing how poets could adapt Latin syntax to the requirements of Old English meter.[48]

Anglo-Latin poetry did not remain a separate tradition from Old English poetry, because the two traditions developed alongside one another. Old English poetry adapts Latin sources, Latin vocabulary, and Latin forms as those things can be translated into the vernacular, and Old English poetry, as we have it, clearly flourished in a multilingual tradition where it may have been composed by the same people who composed verses in Latin. Among the verse forms shared and adapted between the two languages, the verse riddle tradition incorporates the forms of both language traditions. The riddles of Symphosius, composed in North Africa in the fourth century CE, influence the form of Aldhelm's – like Symphosius, Aldhelm composes a collection of riddles, and directly adapts some of Symphosius's riddles in his own collection. The riddle tradition continues through the collections of *enigmata* by Bede, Eusebius, and Boniface, and makes its way into the vernacular in the form of the roughly one hundred riddles in Old English collected in the Exeter Book of Old English poetry. While the Latin riddles introduced their solutions in a title or as an acrostic, Old English poems generally cannot do this: they lack titles, and in the absence of regular line breaks, there are no initial letters to form into a solution. One or two reveal their solutions instead in runes, mimicking Latin acrostic in the same manner as the "Cynewulf" signature

---

[46] Watson, *Balaam's Ass*, I.   [47] Lapidge, *Anglo-Latin Literature*, I.
[48] Reider, "Interlingual Dimensions."

passages, such as the hen riddle, Riddle 40. In general, however, the Old English riddles lack explicit solutions, and indeed lack clear beginnings and endings to the extent that scholars cannot always be entirely sure where one riddle begins and another ends, and thus how many riddles there actually are. Some riddles are, or seem to be, fairly straightforward, and others work to sound like one thing while saying another. Riddles like Exeter Riddle 23, for instance, suggest a salacious double entendre while simultaneously describing a mundane object, an onion:

> Stapol min is steap-heah;   stonde ic on bedde,
> neoþan ruh nat-hwær.   Neþeð hwilum
> ful cyrtenu   ceorles dohtor,
> mod-wlonc meowle,   þæt heo on mec gripeð,
> ræseð mec on reodne,   reafað min heafod,
> fegeð mec on fæsten. (4–9)[49]

> [My column is steep and high; I stand up in bed, hairy somewhere underneath. At times a very lovely daughter of a churl, a high-minded maid, ventures so that she grips me, rushes me in redness, plunders my head, binds me in an enclosed place.]

Some riddles can be solved because they are directly adapted from the Latin riddle tradition, such as the fish-and-river riddle from Symphosius. But while the Latin version tells its story in the third person, the Old English, like many of the other English riddles, appears in the first person, narrated by a speaker concerned with transience and death should its circumstances change and the fish be separated from its river. Riddle 24, usually solved as a Bible or Gospel, follows in many respects the structure of an Old English elegy, beginning in the violence and uncertainty of the world – "[m]ec feonda sum feore besnyþede" (some enemy deprived me of life; 1) – before gradually building to a homiletic conclusion pointing to the end of uncertainty and transience in heaven:

> Gif min bearn wera   brucan willað,
> hy beoð þy gesundran   ond þy sige-fæstran,
> heortan þy hwætran   ond þy hyge-bliþran (18–20)

> [If the children of men wish to enjoy me, they will be thereby healthier and more firm in victory, their hearts thereby bolder and happier in spirit.]

These verses reflect the capaciousness of Old English poetry – homiletic themes and rhetorical parallels combine with the Latinate riddle tradition and incorporate the forms and structure of a vernacular, first-person elegy. The genre of riddling poetry in general asks readers to recognize familiar objects through

---

[49] Riddle texts from Orchard, ed., *Old English and Anglo-Latin Riddle Tradition*.

surprising descriptions of features that might make them seem strange, but the Old English poetic riddle in particular suggests an assumed familiarity with other literary conventions its readers might know.

Verse in early medieval England occurs in both English and Latin, and it draws on literary traditions from continental Europe to northern Africa. It shares cultural references with Old Norse poetry, adapts Old Saxon poetry, moves from Latin to English and back again. And crucially, it exists in manuscripts alongside prose texts, and as we will see, alternates with prose in both adapting Latin prosimetrical texts and making new ones. English verse, even in this earliest moment, is always part of a multilingual tradition, always invested in and interacting with traditions from beyond English shores. Verse forms stretch across time, as well: the Latin meter of early medieval England draws upon the meters available in late antiquity, while the vernacular, English alliterative meter, carries on past the Norman Conquest, changing as grammar changes but retaining a link between the earliest English medieval verse and the latest.

2 Mixed Forms: Prose and Verse

In his *De virginitate*, Aldhelm describes the prose version of his text as the walls of a house and the verse version as the house's roof: "as if the rhetorical foundation-stones were now laid and the walls of prose were built," he intends to next "build a sturdy roof with trochaic slates and dactylic tiles of metre."[50] Although early English authors famously produced rhythmic, alliterating prose (as we will see in the next section), their sense of the distinction between prose and verse nevertheless remained clear: both in Latin and in the vernacular, writers produced prosimetrical texts (including the Old English *Boethius*, or the *Chronicle* poems) that alternated between verse and prose. These texts rely on the formal interplay between these juxtaposed forms. Along these lines, Anglo-Latin writers were the first to adopt and adapt the late antique form of the *opus geminatum*, which pairs "twinned" prose and verse versions of the same text. Aldhelm's *De virginitate*, Bede's *Vita Sancti Cuthberti*, and Alcuin's *Vita Sancti Willibrordi* all exemplify this practice. These overt juxtapositions of verse and prose even occasion explicit comment from their authors on the proper functions of these distinct forms, and thereby may give us a glimpse into cultural expectations for prose and verse forms more broadly. The interplay between verse and prose in both Old English and Anglo-Latin, and the conventional forms that attend upon both, take part in broader literary traditions, too. The roots of the *opus geminatum* tradition begin in antiquity, with the practice of paraphrase known as *conversio*, whereby prose could be turned into metrical verse and verse into

---

[50] Aldhelm, *Aldhelmi Opera Omnia*, 321; Lapidge and Herren, *Aldhelm*, 130–31.

prose.[51] Most directly, early Latin writers in medieval England follow in the footsteps of earlier Christian Latin writers for whom "biblical prose – and especially the Gospels – becomes the subject of metrical paraphrase by poets seeking to supply a wider Christian reading public with literature of sophistication suitable to the tastes acquired studying Virgil and other Latin poets in classical schools."[52] The Spanish priest Juvencus began this practice in the fourth century CE, paraphrasing biblical passages in verse while being sure to maintain strict fidelity to their content. Caelius Sedulius's influential *Carmen* and *Opus paschale* continue in this vein, with the *Carmen* first offering a verse counterpart to the Gospels and the *Opus* then re-paraphrasing the *Carmen*.[53] In one sense, then, we might think of Old English biblical poems like *Genesis A & B*, *Exodus*, *Daniel*, and *Judith* as vernacular manifestations of this same tradition, as counterparts or intertexts across the linguistic divide between Latin and English. As texts continue to be adapted from prose into verse or into prosimetrum, we are offered a rare glimpse into how writers conceived of the different roles of verse and prose forms.

Having come to the end of the prose *De virginitate*, Aldhelm sets out his plan for its poetic sequel. He refers to the foregoing prose as his "rhetorical narratives" and what he will do next as an attempt "with artistry to adorn the renown of this same chastity ... in the heroic measures of hexameter verse."[54] Rhetoric here seems almost to become a third term to prose and meter, the foundational skill underlying but apparently distinct from both forms of composition. But lest the language of "artistry" that "adorns" make it seem that meter merely decorates prose, the metaphor of the house clarifies how all of these things work together: "as if the rhetorical foundation-stones were now laid and the walls of prose were built, so I shall – trusting in heavenly support – build a sturdy roof with trochaic slates and dactylic tiles of metre."[55] The meter must be a sturdy covering for the prose walls of the house, both built upon a foundation of rhetoric. In promising the subsequent composition to the nuns, he entreats in turn to know whether the manner of his prose composition has been "pleasing to your intelligence, particularly since the elegance of metrical beauty and the eloquence of rhetorical disquisition differ as much from each other as sweet new wine is different from heady mead."[56] Aldhelm's reiteration that the style of both his current prose narrative and the verse to come must both be pleasing, offering different kinds of beauty to his audience, does more than just flatter

---

[51] Godman, "The Anglo-Latin *opus geminatum*," 215–17.
[52] Lapidge, *Anglo-Latin Literature*, I, 348.
[53] Godman, "The Anglo-Latin *opus geminatum*," 218.
[54] Lapidge and Herren, *Aldhelm*, 130–31. [55] Lapidge and Herren, *Aldhelm*, 131.
[56] Lapidge and Herren, *Aldhelm*, 131.

those who might receive his work; it suggests an understanding of the importance of affect in both devotional instruction and edification, and importantly does not limit the role of affect and indeed pleasure to one form or the other.

Aldhelm's metaphor of the two parts of his *opus geminatum* as walls and a roof makes an important point about the function of forms: although the roof of a house needs walls to support it, and thus verse perhaps relies on preexisting sturdy prose, the roof of a house is no less structurally essential for those who would like to remain warm, dry, and covered from the elements within those walls. And so although verse may be ornamented, its adornments are not, for Aldhelm, merely decorative or frivolous; they are what the walls exist to uphold. As Thornbury has written, "For [Aldhelm,] as for most early medieval people, to adorn something was not to overlay it with something extraneous, but to transform it through a perceptible manifestation of effort."[57] His understanding of form mirrors his conceptual understanding of virginity as an attribute of those he both describes, and addresses his descriptions to: "Virginity, conceived as an ornament, is thus the end result of a lifelong endeavor, rather than an innate quality preserved by withdrawing from the world."[58] We might recall that Aldhelm paid particular attention to what could be learned from the experience of difficult literary forms, to concealed knowledge and how it could be revealed in new ways. Conveying essentially the same content in multiple forms allows readers to experience that content more fully, from new angles and perspectives that offer better understanding than a single presentation alone.

The earlier, prose version of Aldhelm's *De virginitate* draws upon a treatise on virginity by St. Ambrose of Milan, with some departures. Both texts begin with a consideration of the nature of virginity, followed by a catalogue of virgins; Aldhelm, however, both frames virginity a little differently and includes male virgins in his sprawling catalogue, including Ambrose himself. But scholars have noted that Aldhelm carefully emphasizes chastity alongside virginity, since the audience of nuns at Barking Abbey included those who had previously been married before embarking upon the religious life.[59] In the opening to the prose version, he addresses these women directly, beginning with their abbess Hildelith and several of the prominent nuns among them, moving through an extended simile of their labor compared to that of elite athletes before riffing on Ambrose's metaphor of the industry and community of the bees in a hive, whose "peculiar chastity" resembles the church in being fruitful both in offspring and in honey "innocent of the lascivious coupling of marriage, by means of a certain generative condensation of a very sweet

---

[57] Thornbury, "The Ornament of Virginity," 183.
[58] Thornbury, "The Ornament of Virginity," 183.   [59] Lapidge and Herren, *Aldhelm*, 55–57.

juice."[60] By contrast, the opening of the promised metrical version, the *Carmen de virginitate*, addresses God and the Virgin Mary, describing God as offering protection "from high Olympus" while rejecting the very sort of classical reference this phrasing evokes: "I do not seek verses and poetic measures from the rustic Muses, nor do I seek metrical songs from the Castalian nymphs"; instead, he proclaims his intention to "move the Thunderer [i.e., God]" with prayer.[61] In his prose as in his verse, Aldhelm revels in leisurely sentences and esoteric vocabulary, supplementing the virgins found in Ambrose's earlier catalogue with other figures he sees fit to mention.

A rather different example of an *opus geminatum*, Bede's *Vita Sancti Cuthberti* provides a dense metrical version of an anonymous prose *Vita Sancti Cuthberti*, although Bede went one step further in eventually producing a prose account of Cuthbert's life all his own,[62] thus making both halves of the pair: a twinned work with an older sibling. Although the metrical *Vita Sancti Cuthberti* adds a dozen episodes not present in the anonymous life, its dense style and Bede's retelling of these events in his own prose has led to the metrical version being largely overlooked.[63] But as Lapidge argues, the verse may tell us important things about early Anglo-Latin literary form and about Bede's developing style in particular: a version of the *Vita* in the manuscript Besançon, Bibliothèque municipale 186 reproduces lines from late Latin poets more closely, commits metrical errors, offers incorrect place names, and avoids elision more frequently, while the versions of the poem that survive in the rest of the twenty or so manuscripts of its provenance do not. Revising lines lifted from late Latin poets, smoothing out the scansion, and introducing alliteration between the halves of certain lines, the remaining manuscripts hew more closely to Bede's mature style, suggesting revision by Bede himself, while an early version survives uniquely in the Besançon manuscript.[64] In moving from the metrical to the prose *Vita*, Bede also comments upon the forms of the halves of his *opera geminata*, differing from Aldhelm somewhat in ascribing utility and accessibility to the later prose narrative in particular, declaring that in this version he took care to ascertain his details anew and "certam veritatis indaginem simplicibus explicatam sermonibus commendare membranulis" (to commend to parchment the sure, clear investigation of truth in simple discourse).[65] In this evolving articulation of the roles of both halves of the *opus geminatum*,

---

[60] Lapidge and Herren, *Aldhelm*, 62; see Weston, "Honeyed Words."
[61] Lapidge and Rosier, *Aldhelm*, 103.   [62] Lapidge, *Anglo-Latin Literature*, I, 339.
[63] Lapidge, *Anglo-Latin Literature*, I, 339–40.   [64] Lapidge, *Anglo-Latin Literature*, I, 340–46.
[65] Bede, *Vita Sancti Cuthberti*, in *Venerabilis Bedæ Anglosaxonis Presbyteri Opera Omnia*, ed., Migne, col. 733; Godman, "Anglo-Latin *opus geminatum*," 223.

however, Bede continues to develop a vision of those halves as part of a whole, and this vision would continue to influence how the form was practiced in early medieval England.

The *opus geminatum* tradition carries on as Alcuin adapts Bede's own work, including his prose *Historia ecclesiastica* and the metrical *Vita Sancti Cuthberti* in Alcuin's own *Versus de Sanctis Euboricensis Ecclesiae* (Verses on the Saints of the Church of York). In this practice, he follows Bede's own versification of the earlier prose life of Cuthbert, as well as the versification of the *Vita Sancti Martini* of Venantius Fortunatus, and Sedulius's earlier versification of prose Gospel narrative, providing a "twin" to works he himself had not written. Yet as the form evolved, increasingly "in Anglo-Latin literature the two parts of the *opus geminatum* had come to be regarded as elements of a single whole, whereas to Caelius Sedulius they remained distinct *libelli*."[66] Aldhelm, for instance, clearly assumes knowledge of his prose *De virginitate* and refers to the earlier work in his verse *Carmen de virginitate*. Alcuin presented the two halves of his *Vita Sancti Willibrordi* at the same time, and the early manuscripts of the work present both the verse and prose halves of the work together.[67]

Mixed forms appeared in the vernacular as well, although *opera geminata* in Old English prove somewhat more ambiguous than their Latin counterparts. There exist, of course, verse and prose versions of similar texts. Difficulty arises, in part, from our ignorance of the authors and circumstances of composition of many Old English texts compared to Latin texts from the same period. While, for instance, Aldhelm clearly intended his prose and verse works to go together as twinned works, some Old English versifications of prose works seem only to have been retroactive, rather than "twinned" works intended to be read together. The *Solomon and Saturn*, for one, exists in two versions, and the life of St. Andrew exists in Old English in both verse and prose. But Old English also exhibits use of mixed forms in prosimetrical texts that alternate between prose and verse. The Old English translation of Boethius's *Consolation of Philosophy*, for example, exists both in a version that translates the Latin prosimetrical text into straight prose, and in one that follows the Latin original in alternating between prose and verse.[68] Scholars generally agree that the vernacular prose translation came first, with the prosimetrical version later simply versifying the appropriate sections of the prose, those referred to in the text as having been sung.[69] But this prosimetrical translation also offers a self-conscious commentary

---

[66] Godman, "Anglo-Latin *opus geminatum*," 220.
[67] Godman, "Anglo-Latin *opus geminatum*," 223.
[68] Erica Weaver has suggested that these versions form a kind of *opus geminatum*; see Weaver, "Hybrid Forms."
[69] Godden and Irvine, *The Old English* Boethius, I, 80–92.

on the new incorporation of verse sections in an added verse preface without basis in the Latin. The verse preface suggests that supplementing the existing prose translation with verses has only been done for the *selflic secg*, the "self-regarding man" who would otherwise have trouble paying attention to a dense philosophical text in prose:

> Ðus Ælfred us   ealdspell reahte,
> cyning Westsexna,   cræft meldode,
> leoðwyrhta list.   Him wæs lust micel
> ðæt he ðiossum leodum   leoð spellode,
> monnum myrgen,   mislice cwidas,
> þy læs ælinge   ut adrife
> selflicne secg,   þonne he swlces lyt
> gymð for his gilpe.   Ic sceal giet sprecan,
> fon on fitte,   folccuðne ræd
> hæleðum secgean.   Hliste se þe wille.[70]

[Thus Alfred, the king of the West Saxons, related to us an old story, set forth his craft, the poet his skill. In him was a great desire to relate poetry to these people, delight to men, various sayings, lest boredom drive out the self-regarding man, when he cares little for such because of his arrogance. I shall yet speak, take up verse, tell familiar counsel to men. Let him hear who will.]

Unlike Aldhelm's prose walls and verse roof metaphor, the prose preface to the *Boethius* does not seem to directly acknowledge that the versifying is a necessary part of the structure of the text, but rather suggests that verses serve as a concession to a less sophisticated audience. But there is reason not to take this commentary entirely at face value. For one, the lines adapt another important relevant literary tradition, in echoing the justification Caelius Sedulius offered in a prefatory letter for his *Carmen paschale*, arguing that the versification of biblical content would appeal more readily to those who would otherwise engage less enthusiastically with the content:

> hi quicquid rhetoricae facundiae perlegunt, neglegentius adsequuntur, quoniam illud haud diligunt; quod autem versuum viderit blandimento mellitum tanto cordis aviditate suscipiunt ut in alta memoria saepius haec iterando contituant et reponant.[71]

---

[70] Godden and Irvine, *The Old English* Boethius, I, C-Text, Verse Preface. Traditionally the *Boethius* and other translations of Latin works had been considered as part of a translation project carried out by Alfred the Great himself, although scholars have since raised doubts about both the level of Alfred's involvement and the texts that may be connected to Alfred's court directly; see Godden, "Did King Alfred Write Anything?"

[71] Huemer, ed., *Sedulius Opera Omnia*, 5, lines 6–10.

[Whatever rhetorical eloquence they read, they engage more carelessly, because they do not value it at all; but however when one sees verses sweetened with such embellishment they receive them with such eagerness of the heart that they set and place them in deep memory by repeating them more often.]

Crucially, although these lines seem critical of the more careless (*neglegentius*) engagement of one who fails to love the same edifying content in prose, they do not condemn the delight in the same matter in verse, and consider the eager repetition and keeping of the sweet verses well worth the effort of embellishment. Along those lines, even the figure of "Alfred" in the *Boethius* preface exhibits both desire (*lust micel*) and skill (*list, cræft*) in poetic arts. For another, the prosimetrical form hews more closely to the form of its Latin source, which had subtly deployed different types of meter for different verse sections: while, at the beginning of the work, Boethius laments his fortune in elegiac meter, the rest of his dialogue with *Philosophia* encompasses many different poetic meters, returning to elegiacs only once.[72] Restoring the formal parallels to the extent possible in Old English verse recalls the virtuosic skill Boethius had for poetry as well, setting its "Alfred" in an intellectual line of descent from him. And finally, the translation itself declines to diminish the role of verse, even when questions arise on the use of examples and images to illustrate difficult concepts, or using overtly "eald" (old) and "leas" (false) stories to illustrate truths.[73] Rather, in both suggesting that some of the audience of the text will prove too arrogant or less able to understand its dense philosophical content, and invoking an echo of the biblical injunction "He who has ears to hear, let him hear,"[74] the verse preface implicitly exhorts its audience to receive its instruction with a devotional disposition. However delightful its verses might be, audiences are reminded not to take the work as mere entertainment.

As another collection of verse intermingled with prose, the poems of the *Anglo-Saxon Chronicle* often find themselves anthologized separately with other Old English poems. Yet in the context of their composition, they were part of a complex historical narrative, shaping how the *Chronicle*'s audience understood the events of history. The *Chronicle* proceeds year by year, with many years' entries quite brief: "Her Guðlac se halga forðferde" (Here St. Guthlac died) makes up the entire entry for the year 714, for example.[75] But as the history approaches the *Chronicle* writers' present, or at moments of particular significance, the *Chronicle* accumulates detail, flourish, and critical commentary. Verse

---

[72] Claassen, "Literary *Anamnesis*," 6–8.
[73] Godden and Irvine, *The Old English* Boethius, I, C-Text, Meter 23, lines 7–11, as well as elsewhere throughout the text. See Lorden, "Tale and Parable."
[74] Matt. 13:43.   [75] Irvine, ed., *Anglo-Saxon Chronicle 7: MS. E*, 35.

first appears in the entry for 937 AD, with the poem on *The Battle of Brunanburh*. Some versions of the *Chronicle*, including the late Peterborough Chronicle, simply record the events in conventional prose formula: "AN.dccccxxxvii. Her Æðelstan cyning lædde fyrde to Brunanbyrig" (937 AD: Here King Aethelstan led an army to Brunanburh).[76] The version surviving in the "A" manuscript, the Winchester Chronicle thought to be the earliest of the surviving chronicles, however, breaks into a narrative of the battle related in Old English verse. In this context, appearing particularly in the early, southern manuscripts of the *Chronicle*, a poem like *The Battle of Brunanburh* becomes part of the celebration and promotion of the West Saxon kings to whose benefit the early *Chronicle* copies were made.[77]

Some of the so-called poems are brief, a sudden burst of poetry upon the progress of the narrative. The poem on *The Death of Edgar* appears in the three "southern" manuscripts of the *Chronicle*. Yet even the post-Conquest Peterborough Chronicle does include verse at this point, although that verse has been dismissed as "substitut[ing] for the poem short passages on the same subjects in prose or irregular meter."[78] The entry in Peterborough containing verses on *The Death of Edgar* takes the conventional prose formulation for the death of a ruler, "Her ___ gefor" (Here ___ passed), as the first half line of a poem, continuing in and out of verse through the events attendant upon his death:

> Her Eadgar gefor   Angla reccent
> Westseaxna wine   7 Myrcene mundbora.
> Cuð wæs þet wide   geond feola þeoda
> þet aferan Eadmundes   ofer ganetes bað
> cyningas hine wide   wurðodon side,
> bugon to cyninge   swa wæs him gecynde.[79]

> [Here Edgar passed, the ruler of the Angles, the friend of the West Saxons and protector of Mercia. That was widely known throughout many peoples that kings honored him, the offspring of Edmund, far and wide, over the gannet's bath, bowed to the king, as was fitting to them.]

The verses relating the death of a king, naming him in terms of his parentage, recalling how widely known he was among kings over whom he held sway, recall the opening lines of *Beowulf* that relate the greatness of Scyld Scefing retroactively from the event of his funeral. The formulaic poetic phrase "ofer ganotes bæð" (over the gannet's bath), referring to the expanse of the sea,

---

[76] Irvine, ed., *Anglo-Saxon Chronicle 7: MS. E*, 55.   [77] See Smith, "Edgar Poems," 105.
[78] Krapp and Dobbie, eds., *Anglo-Saxon Poetic Records*, vol. VI, 105–6.
[79] Irvine, ed., *The Anglo-Saxon Chronicle 7: MS. E*, 59.

appears in line 1861 of *Beowulf*, as Hrothgar pledges the continuation of mutual friendship with Beowulf's people, a loyalty not diminished by the expanse of the sea between them. But as the *Chronicle* continues in conventional prose, as "Eadward Eadgares sunu feng to rice" (Edward, Edgar's son, came to power), more unconventional signs and portents come about: notably the "cometa se steorra" (the comet star) appears, followed by hunger and unrest.[80] The conventional verses seemingly recognize Edgar as a king in the model of heroic verse, and as his rule gives way, poetry gives way to unsettling prose. While Scott Thompson Smith has crucially argued that the poems on Edgar's coronation and on his death be read "as discrete texts, each one with its own aesthetic character and function attributable to its different historical circumstances,"[81] poems like these also challenge our idea of what constitutes a text. Modern ideas of literature and authorship encourage us to think of texts as singular productions, by a particular person at a particular time, in a definitive form reproduced and experienced similarly by all readers. But the *Chronicle*, and the verses it contains in particular, are both singular productions and mutable ones. Individual texts may be added as a new entry for each year, and the work becomes a shifting whole into which new material was continually absorbed. When we widen the frame to consider not just the two Edgar poems but the prose entries surrounding them, the *Chronicle* becomes a commentary on itself, qualifying the glory of the beginning of Edgar's reign with grim knowledge and eloquent nostalgia at its end.

The final of the six *Chronicle* poems included in the standard edition *Anglo-Saxon Poetic Records* is *The Death of Alfred*, a poem described by E.V.K. Dobbie as "not regularly alliterative, like the other five poems, but ... partly prose and partly irregular rimed verse."[82] This poem does not appear in the earliest two versions of the *Chronicle* (which end with the entries for 975 and 977, respectively).[83] The entry opens with a stylized prose passage, heralding Alfred "se unceððiga æþeling" (the innocent prince), before moving into lines that combine rhyme and intermittent alliteration on strong metrical positions as they relate the story of the prince's blinding at the behest of Earl Godwin:

> Sona swa he **lende**, on scype man hine **blende**,
> and hine swa **bli**ndne brohte to ðam munecon,
> and he þar wun**ode** ða hwile þe he lyf**ode**.
> Syððan hine man **byrigde**, swa him wel **gebyrede**,
> ful **wurð**lice, swa he **wyrð**e wæs.[84]

---

[80] Irvine, ed., *The Anglo-Saxon Chronicle 7: MS. E*, 59. [81] Smith, "Edgar Poems," 109.
[82] Dobbie, ed., *Anglo-Saxon Poetic Records*, VI, xxxii.
[83] Dobbie, ed., *Anglo-Saxon Poetic Records*, VI, xxxvii.
[84] Dobbie, ed., *Anglo-Saxon Poetic Records*, VI, 24–25; emphasis added.

[As soon as he came to land, men blinded him on the ship, and thus blind brought him to the monks, and he dwelled there as long as he lived. After he was buried, as well befitted him, very worthily, as he was worthy.]

While the rhyming verbs in the first half of the poem reiterate the litany of evils carried out by Godwin, the pummeling rhyme in its latter half emphasizes the particular violence and effects of this violence wrought upon the body of the innocent prince, who lives out his short life among monks and receives a burial befitting his station and innocence, both emphasized in contrast to the violence carried out by Godwin. The verse of the Peterborough Chronicle thus traces both history and the changes in poetic form leading up to and following the Norman Conquest. Although later *Chronicle* poems are excluded from Dobbie's edition as being both "later" and "in irregular meter," they show us how English verse continued to evolve across the Conquest.[85] *Chronicle* verse forms move from a battle poem like *Brunanburh*, an Old English elegiac poem with martial imagery in alliterative meter, through *The Death of Alfred*, to a rhyming poem on William the Conqueror, embodying in its form the depth of change the Conquest wrought.[86]

Although many of the traditions of mixed forms, from *opera geminata* to prosimetrical texts, in early medieval England flowed from Latin into the vernacular, English texts were also adapted into Latin, as well. One instance that allows us to see the workings of mixed prose and verse forms across languages is the *Chronicon* of Æthelweard, which largely follows the *Anglo-Saxon Chronicle* and even adapts its English verse into Latin. Although the *Chronicle* poems only begin in the 900s and Æthelweard's *Chronicon* ends with the entry for 975, we can see, at least, how an English writer adapted the highly conventional poems on the coronation and death of Edgar into the conventions of Latin verse. The poem on the coronation of Edgar takes its time in approaching the king; it begins instead with a complex reckoning of time in units of "Septimanas recitant post quas nunc uoce Latini" (what Latinists now at a later time call "septimanae").[87] Then follows a conventional invocation of the muses: "Tingite nunc calamo, Musae, propriumque uocate/ Carmen, et ignoto uentis properate secundis" (Imbue now from your reed pen, Oh Muses, call the song your own, and hasten with following winds the ignorant one).[88] Only then does the prince (called by the Greek term "Anax") come to power, in front of the thronging troops and nameless crowds he governs. In prose, the Latin *Chronicon* then notes only the date of the year before launching into the poem

---

[85] Dobbie, ed., *Anglo-Saxon Poetic Records*, VI, xxxii–xxxiii.
[86] Trilling, *Aesthetics of Nostalgia*, 241.   [87] Campbell, ed., *Chronicle of Æthelweard*, 55.
[88] Campbell, ed., *Chronicle of Æthelweard*, 55.

on Edgar's death. The prose expresses the year straightforwardly in years since the birth of Christ, "annorum numerus nongentesimus et supra septuagesimus adhaerensque ternus" (the number of years nine hundred and seventy more and additionally three [i.e., 973]).[89] But as prose turns to poetry again, the reckoning of time reverts to mathematical formulas of groups of years, suggesting that the measurement of time in verse has to occur differently.

Writers in early medieval England made the most of their ability to alternate between prose and verse, and between different kinds of prose and verse forms. Texts that juxtapose prose and verse also sometimes occasion comment on how these forms are understood, the different but overlapping roles played by prose and verse, and writers have different things to say on this account. Latin writers like Aldhelm framed verse and prose as different parts of a whole structure, while in English, versification receives apology in some ways rhetorically similar to apologies for translation – a concession to those who need it – that may be more conventional than earnest, as the verses created therefrom recombine poetic and other conventions to evoke new associations. That parallel may be significant not least because some Old English verse does indeed both translate and versify Latin prose texts, particularly biblical texts and saints' lives. In Latin, early English writers stood in a long tradition of *opera geminata*, prosimetra, and versifications of sacred texts, and they made this clear through their overt borrowings from late Latin writers. Latin is adapted into Old English, and prose into verse. The meeting of forms in these texts tells us about the varied cultural functions early English writers thought formal conventions could perform, what flourishes and references were most fitting to similar content in different formal contexts. It shows us, too, how Latinate conventions migrate and transform across centuries and across the linguistic divide between Anglo-Latin and Old English, and how functionally similar forms might be rhetorically positioned differently in the texts that contain them.

3 Prose Forms

Prose might, in Aldhelm's formulation, provide the walls that hold up the roof of meter. But this by no means suggests that verse merely decorates more humdrum prose, nor that prose functions without its own aesthetic style. This section considers the various ways that prose forms in early medieval England offered much more than a little flourish on their otherwise bland content – although as we will see later, plain style had its purposes, too. The rhythmic prose of Old English homilies and saints' lives, in particular, and the arcane vocabulary of hermeneutic Latin offer two kinds of ornamented prose with distinct functional goals.

---

[89] Campbell, ed., *Chronicle of Æthelweard*, 55.

Alliterative, rhythmic prose in the vernacular – notably that of Ælfric and Wulfstan – might offer vivid and memorable exposition to both lay and monastic readers, offering their learned content to a community of believers with widely varying levels of literary and exegetical skill. Anonymous vernacular homilies are far from staid in their style, either, incorporating images and aural effects shared with the stock of vernacular poetry. At the same time, the obscure language and complex syntax of hermeneutic Latin prose – such as that of Aldhelm early in the period or Byrhtferth of Ramsey later in the period – created a community of a different kind: a community that shared an elite level of education and understanding, and that possessed the skill to decipher these esoteric texts. Aside from their stylized language, prose texts, not unlike poetic texts, also make use of structural elements that frame how their content should be read and understood. These structural elements include highly conventional prologues or epilogues, establishing the connections between authors and audiences, or between audiences and broader communities, between present and past, or between the text and various kinds of authority. Attending to the forms of prose helps us to understand how prose texts performed various functions in early English literary culture beyond simply conveying content.

In the vernacular, the two most-discussed bodies of pre-Conquest prose are the ninth-century translation projects traditionally connected to Alfred the Great of Wessex, and prose homilies, including the works of the great tenth-century homilists, Ælfric and Wulfstan. But both bodies of prose take their place in larger histories of related vernacular prose and longer traditions of Latin learning. Ælfric, for one, draws heavily on the work of Paul the Deacon, Haymo, and Smaragdus, while Blickling Homily I translates an African Christmas Homily.[90] Wulfstan, in turn, draws heavily on Ælfric. The so-called "Alfredian" texts, meanwhile, take a range of approaches to adapting their Latin sources, often interweaving and interjecting material from glosses, other philosophical works, and apparently original illustrative metaphors in order to make those texts live anew in translation. Vernacular prose texts are associated with named authors more often than vernacular poetry, although questions of authorship and influence remain complicated, as we shall see. While we might tend to think of prose language as stylistically unmarked, as opposed to poetic language, early English writing in both Old English and Latin evinces both careful stylistic choices and notable formal conventions.

Ælfric's homilies are known for deploying a densely alliterative, rhythmic prose. The fact that the homilies and saints' lives of Ælfric unfold in a distinctive, alliterating compositional style has led scholars to consider

---

[90] Clayton, "Homiliaries and Preaching in Anglo-Saxon England," 161; Fiedler, "Sources," 122–24.

whether they might break down the boundary between verse and prose altogether.[91] But as Weiskott has demonstrated, these alliterating prose patterns do not adhere to the remarkably consistent metrical patterns discussed in Section 1.[92] They do, however, accomplish a memorable, compelling cadence suited both for private reading and oral delivery. Although Ælfric's prose may not fulfill the requirements of vernacular meter, his style does suggest a concern with an audience that might respond best to aural features that delight, and language that might aid the memory in engaging with and holding onto a particular turn of phrase – indeed, not unlike the function imagined for prosimetrical texts and *opera geminata*.

Ælfric was a product of the Benedictine Reforms of the tenth century, when Benedictine monks led by Æthelwold, bishop of Winchester, Dunstan, the Archbishop of Canterbury, and Oswald, the Archbishop of York, made efforts to expel secular (i.e., non-monastic) clergy from ecclesiastical centers and replace them with monastic authorities and institutions influenced by continental practices.[93] As a student of Æthelwold's Winchester in particular, Ælfric both reflects and departs from the linguistic practices of the Benedictine Reformers in important ways. The Reformers produced numerous texts in Old English prose, including an Old English translation of the Benedictine Rule. As Rebecca Stephenson has argued, the straightforward prose they valued in the vernacular was balanced by and contrasted with their use of a Latin style reminiscent of the hermeneutic Latin of the eighth century.[94] Ælfric nonetheless evinces a generally straightforward style in both his Old English and his Latin writings, as we will see in the next section, contrasting with the often more complex Latin styles of his Benedictine colleagues. But understanding Ælfric's work requires considering the context in which he wrote them – after leaving Winchester he wrote from Cerne Abbas, producing works under the patronage of wealthy laypersons who possessed a functional knowledge of Latin but wanted access to monastic teaching in their own tongue.[95] However we understand them, his stylistic choices would seem to reflect his concern for the edification of the audiences for whom he wrote.

Just as translation from Latin into Old English prose flourished, new prose was, of course, composed in Anglo-Latin throughout the early medieval period, as we have seen. Anglo-Latin prose forms varied, while the complex hermeneutic Latin tradition extended from Aldhelm in the seventh century to Byrhtferth of Ramsey in the eleventh. While style occupies part of the next

---

[91] Bredehoft, *Early English Metre*; Beechy, *Poetics of Old English*.
[92] Weiskott, *English Alliterative Verse*, 10–13. [93] Blair, *Church in Anglo-Saxon Society*, 142.
[94] Stephenson, *Politics of Language*. [95] Cubitt, "Ælfric's Lay Patrons," 165–66.

section as well, Byrhtferth's style deserves particular attention here because of the ways that he moves between the hermeneutic style and more straightforward Latin prose, particularly in his *Enchiridion*, which alternates a more accessible Latin style with short passages of hermeneutic Latin.[96] As Stephenson shows, particularly in the wake of the Benedictine monastic reforms of the tenth century, different types and registers of language were used to very different social and political ends. Hermeneutic Latin, accessible only to more highly educated monks, and generally less so to lower level clerics or educated laypeople who would have had more basic knowledge of Latin, served to linguistically reinforce the monastic identity of those who could access and understand the texts it comprised – as she puts it, the Reformers' "political context . . . encouraged the simultaneous development of a simple English style and an esoteric Latin style."[97] While one served to emphasize the rarefied heights of learned authority the monks occupied, the other served to emphasize their role in using that authority to instruct those who lived under it. But the fact that not only those who were subject to the monks might need somewhat more accessible prose from time to time is evidenced in part by the varieties of Latin prose style deployed by the monks.

Latin prose also allowed English writers to create works that might be read outside of English shores, and allowed foreigners to write Latin works for English readers. One such work was Lantfred's *Translatio Sancti Swithuni*, by a Benedictine monk originally from Fleury who came to Winchester during the time of the Benedictine Reform.[98] In composing the life of an English bishop (although not one who was a monk himself, as Lantfred's text carefully neglects to mention) he imports the continental form of the miracle collection to valorize an English saint about whose life nothing was known. Framing his text from the outset as one made in service to the Benedictine Reformers at Winchester, Lantfred makes the challenge in writing the life of a saint whose life was unknown part of his point – as he presents it, only the wickedness of the secular clerics allowed Swithun's deeds to be forgotten, and only the holiness of the Reformers has allowed his miracles now to come to light. The miracle stories related are largely archetypal miracles – the kind that, as E. Gordon Whatley has argued, make their point precisely through being as much like recognizable miracle stories from the gospels and lives of other saints as possible, with little distinction to suggest any difference or distance between them.[99] When

---

[96] Baker and Lapidge, eds., *Byrhtferth's Enchiridion*.
[97] Stephenson, *The Politics of Language*, 5; as well as Stephenson, "Ælfric of Eynsham and Hermeneutic Latin," 112n6.
[98] Lapidge, ed. and trans., *Cult of St Swithun*, 217–334. [99] Whatley, "Lost in Translation."

Ælfric adapts this text into English, we can see changes to both form and content responsive to a different linguistic and textual context.[100] Although Ælfric writes a prose style intended to be accessible, it is anything but plain, even when it is concise; he writes to move his hearers as well as instruct them. In explaining the reason for his English writing, he overtly nods toward the divisions between learned monastic authorities and those in their care.[101] Because these statements follow both the political and social lines of Ælfric's milieu as well as conventional statements about translation, we should read them less as expressions of personal concern than as formal, and indeed formulaic, rhetorical gestures to be made in this sort of prose text.[102] Ælfric's warnings, then, when some bit of the monastic learning he conveys might present particularly tantalizing or challenging elements, also serve to reinforce those hierarchies and identities while also limiting potential dangers, as when he is forced to relate one of numerous prophetic dreams in his adaptation of Lantfred's life of Swithun:

> Nu is to witenne þæt we ne sceolan cepan ealles to swyðe be swefnum forðan þe he ealle ne beoð of gode . Sume swefna syndon soðlice of gode swa swa we on bocum rædað and sume beoð of deofle to sumum swicdom hu he ða sawle forwære ... god sylf forbead þæt we swefnum ne folgion þe læs ðe se deofol us bedydrian mæge.[103]

> [Now it is to be known that we should not at all regard dreams too greatly because they are not all from God. Some dreams are truly from God just as we read in books, and some are from the devil for the purpose of some deceit, how he may hinder the soul ... God himself forbade that we should follow dream lest the devil may delude us.]

This interjection, with no precedent in Lantfred's original, validates the stories of prophetic dreams sanctioned by monastic and explicitly literate authority (including, implicitly, his own) while generally proscribing such experiences for an audience lacking such authority themselves.

Often beginning with Latin versions imported to England, saints' lives may be translated into Old English prose, before sometimes being translated again into Old English verse. Even when the early English began writing and commissioning the lives of their homegrown saints, those English saints' lives often began in Latin versions,[104] as in the case of Lantfred's life of Swithun mentioned earlier. In fact, in the case of Swithun, Ælfric pointedly attributes his account of a local English saint to a foreign authority in Latin – "land-ferð se

---

[100] Skeat, ed., *Ælfric's Lives of Saints*, I, 440–71.   [101] Stephenson, *Politics of Language*.
[102] Gittos, "Audience for Old English Texts."
[103] Skeat, ed., *Ælfric's Lives of Saints*, I, 466, lines 403–7, 412–13.
[104] Kramer, Magennis, and Norris, eds. and trans., *Anonymous Old English Lives of Saints*, ix.

ofer-sæwisca" (Lantfred the foreigner).[105] Yet while Ælfric professes to say nothing in his vernacular life of Swithun that he had not found "gefyrn awriten on ledenbocum" (previously written in Latin books),[106] he makes several more subtle changes to the details he had found there, lessening the crimes of persons whose punishments were erased by the saint, replacing female recipients of miracles with male ones, and removing a particularly spectacular anecdote about a man afflicted by female demons.[107] Clearly, although the invocation of Lantfred's Latinate authority offers both conventional and particular validation of the narrative, the different linguistic and social context of Ælfric's vernacular life demanded different conventions and conventional details from the Latin. Famously, many of Ælfric's writings were adapted by Wulfstan, homilist and Archbishop of York. But Wulfstan makes subtle lexical changes to Ælfric's homilies, much as Ælfric had reframed Lantfred's saint's life, reflecting his very different legal and political role as not only a higher-level ecclesiastical figure but an author of law codes for both Æthelstan and Cnut, incorporating, for instance, the Scandinavian word for law (*lagu*) rather than the English (*æ*).[108] For both Ælfric and Wulfstan, vernacular prose style, from the structures of their texts to their aural effects, was integral to the complex ways that their texts functioned in the changing world of the late tenth and early eleventh centuries.

Long before Ælfric and Wulfstan, however, earlier medieval English writers collected prose homilies, whose forms evolved over the course of the period. Homilies are short texts, but most often traveled in larger collections or homiliaries. The uses of these collections varied with place and time, from homiliaries designed for use in the monastic office to those designed for preaching to the laity to those used for monks' private devotional reflection – and as Mary Clayton has shown, "boundaries between genres must have been quite fluid" when it comes to these collections.[109] Prose homilies also accompanied verse texts in the manuscripts that house them, as in the case of the twenty-three Vercelli homilies that take their place in the Vercelli Book, best known as one of the four major codices of Old English poetry. Homilies exhibit their own distinctive conventional forms, yet often share these conventional forms with vernacular verse. In the Vercelli book, a version of the Old English *Soul and Body* poem, in which a damned and blessed soul each visit and speak to the remains of the bodies they inhabited in life, appears in the same manuscript as Vercelli Homily IV, which features a similar conceit in an imaginative narrative

---

[105] Skeat, ed., *Ælfric's Lives of Saints*, I, 466, line 402.
[106] Skeat, ed., *Ælfric's Lives of Saints*, I, 4, line 48.
[107] Lorden, "Landscapes of Devotion," 306.   [108] Stanley, "Wulfstan and Ælfric," 430, 435.
[109] Clayton, "Homiliaries and Preaching in Anglo-Saxon England," 161.

episode in a prose homily. While Vercelli's *Soul and Body* poem depicts souls' predicting whether their bodies would find shame or glory at the day of judgment, Homily IV takes place at that very moment, as a blessed soul exclaims, "Ic gesio hwær min lichama stent on midre þisse menigo. Lætaþ hine to me" (I see where my body stands in the middle of this crowd. Let him come to me!).[110] Both poem and homily note the ravages of worms on the dead body, damage undone now at the resurrection. The curious literary topos of a soul who condemns or applauds the actions of its body in life, separated at death and reunited in either grief or joy at the end of the world, seems to have accrued meaning across the various texts in which it appeared. Alongside Ælfric's and Wulfstan's homilies and the Vercelli homilies, the Blickling Homilies form another major collection of early vernacular homilies. The collection offers an apparently incomplete series of 18 homilies from various authors, evincing Anglian and Mercian linguistic features, archaic language and missing material in at least the beginning and end of the collection as well as major feast days.[111] Clayton has suggested Carolingian parallels in the organization of the collection, which ranges across "Gospel exegesis, sermon, and saint's life."[112] As each of these collections demonstrates, crucial formal insights into early medieval English homilies are found not only in the homilies themselves but also in the structures of the collections that contain them.

Perhaps because of their use for a broad audience – including, but not limited to, laypersons or parish priests and their congregants – prose devotional texts in English often contain built-in structures to guide how they are read and understood, including metacritical comments and narrative framing devices. Prose texts come in a variety of genres, and prose narrative borrows and reflects formal conventions from a variety of genres. Saints' lives in particular allow us to trace the shifting conventions of language and genre, since they tend to exist in many forms. In the case of the Benedictine Reformers, the provenance of a saint's life is often easy to trace, from one named author to another. But numerous anonymous prose saints' lives circulate as well that contain elements that might have seemed surprising if not scandalous to a writer like Ælfric. The Old English life of Saint Christopher, for instance, relates the story of a saint with the head of a dog.[113] The Old English *Life of Malchus* opens with a frame narrative in the first person, carefully emphasizing the themes of chastity, before

---

[110] Scragg, ed., *The Vercelli Homilies and Related Texts*, Homily IV. On the distinctive conventions of the vernacular soul and body tradition in early medieval England, see Lorden, *Forms of Devotion in Early English Poetry*.

[111] Clayton, "Homiliaries and Preaching in Anglo-Saxon England," 167–68.

[112] Clayton, "Homiliaries and Preaching in Anglo-Saxon England," 168.

[113] Fulk, ed., *The* Beowulf *Manuscript*, 1–13; see Kim, "Dog-Headed Saint Christopher."

leaving first person narration (borrowed from its source text in a Latin version by St. Jerome) behind as the narrative proper begins. The structuring device of framing Malchus and his wife as older pilgrims, having nearly completed their life's sacrifice and duty, qualifies the potentially salacious elements of the story about which readers might otherwise be left in tantalizing – potentially too tantalizing – suspense, as Malchus in his younger days leaves the monastery behind, and finds himself captured and forced into enslavement and marriage with "seo þe wæs oðres gemæcca" (she who was the spouse of another).[114] But before we meet Malchus and his wife at all, two other tales from Jerome appear as prologue and perhaps initial buffer, both considering the themes of sexual temptation and the importance of vows. The first relates a devil's temptation of a devout hermit, who isolates himself in the Egyptian wilderness to pray. He admits a prostitute who disguises herself as a woman in distress, and when overcome with lust for her, cannot feel the comparatively milder burning of his fingers held to the flame of a candle.[115] The grisly exemplum leaves no doubt about the extremity to which sexual indulgence ought to be resisted by the truly devout. Such structural framing becomes all the more significant when we consider a similar device in another prose narrative with a devotional purpose but potentially salacious content: the life of *St. Mary of Egypt*, transmitted with but stylistically distinct from the rather more staid homilies of Ælfric. The story begins with Zosimus, a monk since boyhood who overconfidently wonders whether any man can teach him anything else about monastic devotion.[116] As the story goes, however, it will be a woman who teaches him what his cloistered brothers cannot. Zosimus at first does not understand when he encounters Mary naked in the desert, at first erroneously associating her black skin with a demonic presence, but then realizing that she is a woman, modestly attempting to hide her form since she has lost even the clothes on her back in her years of grueling devotion. When they are able to speak, she reveals how starkly her current state of bodily deprivation contrasts with the sensual indulgence she had practiced in her youth. With this context firmly in place, readers approach her story of prolific debauchery only from the point of view of her older self, for whom the contrast offers not prurient interest but the profundity of her conversion and miraculous existence. Her eremitic existence of self-deprivation could not contrast more sharply with the version of her younger self who departed for the holy land only in hope of fornicating with the others on the boat.

---

[114] Dendle, ed. and trans., "The Old English 'Life of Malchus' (Part 2)," 644.
[115] Dendle, ed. and trans., "The Old English 'Life of Malchus' (Part 2)," 633.
[116] Kramer, Magennis, and Norris, eds. and trans., *Anonymous Old English Lives of Saints*, 379–439.

But not all narrative contains such framing devices, even narrative that may have had moral purposes. The Old English *Apollonius of Tyre* circulates with saints' litanies and devotional poems in the vernacular, but the text itself tosses its audience into the midst of a startling narrative about an incestuous king. The text is, by no means, morally ambiguous on this point – the king's own daughter speaks movingly and at some length about her suffering, although the text quickly leaves her behind, without recourse. But as the narrative introduces its protagonist, the Apollonius who learns humility through difficult turns of fortune, the narrative also introduces his pride, wealth, loss of those things, a story of a brothel and a beautiful daughter (although part of the text is missing at this point) and finally, pagan priestesses. Without overt commentary such as that contained in, for example, the Old English *Boethius* when it introduces generally rather tamer stories drawn from pagan antiquity, the *Apollonius* might seem a surprising text for early English translators to have left largely unqualified and intact, and for early English scribes to have copied alongside more overtly devotional texts. But one thing the *Apollonius* does do is demonstrate its protagonists' learning virtue and humility from hard experience. In its historical moment, it may also have served as a careful warning against consanguinity.[117] These Christian virtues, even if framed in pagan terms, might have served as enough of a moral on their own to render the entertaining story edifying in that context.

Slightly different concerns frame the prose associated with the so-called "Alfredian" translation program of the ninth century. First among these is the Old English translation of Gregory the Great's *Cura pastoralis*, or *Pastoral Care*, featuring a famous preface written in the voice of the king himself. In it, the voice of "Alfred" lays out the vision and requirements for a program of translating other such works, those "most necessary for men to know."[118] Malcolm Godden has shown that there exists little evidence connecting most of the works traditionally attributed to Alfred to the king himself, or even to the program envisioned by the *Pastoral Care* preface. Yet the fact remains that there exists a substantial body of prose translated from Latin works, generally localizable to southern England in the late ninth and tenth centuries, that connect themselves, often in prologues or other metatextual apparatus, to the figure of Alfred the Great. Beyond this, however, there remains tremendous variation between the texts themselves, the kinds of Latin prose they translate, and the kinds and levels of learning represented therein. Translated works such as the *Pastoral Care* and the Old English translation of Bede's *Historia*

---

[117] Morini, "Apollonius and Wulfstan," 65–67, 69–76.
[118] Sweet, ed., *Pastoral Care*, Prose Preface, 7.

ecclesiastica might indeed be considered ecclesiastical works, "most needful" for a layperson or parish priest with a basic education to learn from. Yet other texts associated with the figure of Alfred, like the Old English *Boethius* or the translation of Augustine's *Soliloquies*, contain more challenging philosophical concepts, raising questions about human will and the nature of good and evil and cosmology and metaphysics that might prove at least opaque, if not potentially misleading, for readers inadequately prepared for the concepts that they contain. As Godden points out, Alfred's biographer, Asser, does not connect any translated works with the king aside from that of Gregory's *Dialogues*, which he attributes to the bishop Wærferth rather than to Alfred himself.[119] Moreover, "ventriloquizing" in the voice of a king or even a high-status layperson was common in the period, both in contemporaneous texts written in the service of the reputation of the person in question, and often in works written retroactively, that gained some authority by associating themselves with authoritative figures.[120]

Yet there are enough correspondences between the texts to tell us other things. Correspondences in terminology strongly suggest that common authorship for the Old English *Boethius* and *Soliloquies* is "impossible to resist."[121] The Old English *Soliloquies* adapts a source with a similar structure to the *Boethius* – a dialogue between its protagonist and an abstract figure. In the *Boethius*, the *Philosophia* figure of the Latin usually becomes "*Wisdom*" in the English, although sometimes the text uses *Gesceadwisnes*, Reason, the same term used to translate *Ratio*, Reason, throughout the *Soliloquies*. The *Soliloquies'* dialogue, in both Latin and Old English, takes the form of prose throughout. But the Old English version varies wildly in how closely or freely it adapts the Latin, incorporating other Latin sources and both language and ideas from the *Consolation of Philosophy* before, finally, it adds an entire third book not attested in the Latin source. The added book adapts other Augustinian material along with ideas from such sources as Julian of Toledo and Gregory the Great – sources like those named in the translation's prologue as great authorities set in place by God, the ultimate authority, upon whose wisdom another author might draw.[122] As Milton McC. Gatch characterized it, the first book might be considered "as a free paraphrase of the Latin original, the second book is more remotely linked to Augustine's text, and the third (for which there

---

[119] Godden, "Did King Alfred Write Anything?" 3, 12.
[120] Godden, "Did King Alfred Write Anything?" 4–6.
[121] Godden and Irvine, *The Old English* Boethius, I, 136; see also Lockett, *Augustie's Soliloquies*, xv.
[122] Lockett, *Augustine's Soliloquies*, xv–xvi.

is no equivalent in the Latin *Soliloquia*) seems to depart absolutely both from Augustine's argument and from the issue he had posed."[123]

The elaborative, even associative, approach of the Old English *Soliloquies* can be seen in the extended opening metaphor of its prologue, written in the voice of the translator rather than of "Agustinus," that compares the process of translating to that of constructing, to gathering up varied timber and materials to be set "to ælcum þara weorca þe ic wyrcan cuðe" (to every work that I knew how to make). Urging others to the same practice of gathering as much good timber as they can, he proclaims,

> On ælcum treowo ic geseah hwæthwugu þæs þe ic æt ham beþorfte. Forþam ic lære ælcne ðara þe maga si and manigne wæn hæbbe, þæt he menige to þam ilcan wuda þar ic þas studansceaftas cearf. Fetige hym þar ma and gefeðrige hys wænas mid fegrum gerdum, þat he mage windan manigne smicerne wah, and manig ænlic hus settan, and fegerne tun timbrian.[124]

> [On every tree I saw something that I had need for at home. Therefore I teach everyone who may be strong and have many wagons, that he should turn his purposes to that same wood where I cut those sturdy beams. Let him fetch more for himself there and fill his wagons with fair branches, that he may weave many intricate walls, and establish many excellent houses, and build a fair habitation.]

The prologue sets out a clear meaning for this metaphor – whatever the speaker builds, he builds by the grace of the maker of the woods and of himself, God. All the building he does serves the purpose "ge her nytwyrde to beonne, ge huru þider to cumane" (both to be useful here, and indeed to come there).[125] But it also sets out the translation's method and philosophy – gathering pieces of learning from various sources, what the translator considers the best and most useful, to rebuild the *Soliloquies* into something that upholds but also reinforces and embellishes its source. For this reason, some scholars have suggested that the preface introduces a text more like a *florilegium*, a sort of textual collage of passages of wisdom drawn from various authorities and compiled for later use.[126]

Even this level of liberty with an authoritative text demonstrates a complicated negotiation with and reliance upon established authorities. The new material comes from different authorities, and the position of Augustine himself, as author and protagonist of the *Soliloquies*, is altered in the Old English translation. In the original work, Augustine wrote at the moment of his retreat

---

[123] Gatch, "King Alfred's Version of Augustine's *Soliloquia*," 199.
[124] Lockett, *Augustine's Soliloquies*, 182.   [125] Lockett, *Augustine's Soliloquies*, 184.
[126] Whitelock, "The Prose of Alfred's Reign," 71.

before his baptism; the dialogue with his own *Ratio* about the status of the incorporeal soul and the preservation of selfhood in the Christian afterlife apparently represents the questions that consumed him at the moment that he was moving from Manichaeism to Christianity.[127] The Old English translation, however, ascribes to this *Agustinus* the status of bishop, granting him the status of authority retroactively, and, more importantly, the status of one responsible for teaching and edifying others less advanced in the faith rather than only a nascent believer himself.[128] The authority of this bishop *Agustinus* at the start of the text forms a bookend with the ascribed authority of Alfred, who in the *explicit* or ending remarks of the text is named as "compiler, not ... author or translator," as Lockett has pointed out.[129] In so doing, the Old English *Soliloquies* also use prefatory, concluding, and interjected material to help frame the audience's understanding of a potentially difficult text that might raise challenging questions, ones that might raise doubts about central tenets of Christian faith. While the Latin sources of the *Soliloquies* and many translations like it come from beyond English shores, they nevertheless represent crucial attestations of what early English people read and what texts influenced their thought, as well as representing in themselves instances of reading those texts and adapting them innovatively in their own cultural moment. The forms of these translations, moreover, testify to the complexities of their reading and adaptation.

Making broad statements about prose forms in early medieval England can be difficult, because prose was put to such different uses in different contexts and in both Latin and English across the first centuries of English writing. Focusing primarily on the fraught category of literary prose, we can see texts written in various registers, with different levels of accessibility to different audiences. In Latin, early English prose at times deployed difficult and dense hermeneutic Latin, designed to showcase the level of learning required to be in the elite crowd of monastics who could write or even understand it. But in other contexts, early medieval English writers used Latin as the lingua franca that would allow their writings to have currency beyond their shores, to a broader audience of Christian readers on the continent and beyond. In the vernacular, English prose was no less complex. Writers like Ælfric used various prose styles, including rhythmic, alliterating lines of prose that set out to entrance their hearers and work edifying material into their memories. Doing so, he built upon, and departed from, existing prose narrative traditions that rendered homilies and lives of saints

---

[127] Gatch, "King Alfred's Version of Augustine's *Soliloquia*," 203.
[128] Lockett, *Augustine's Soliloquies*.   [129] Lockett, *Augustine's Soliloquies*, 302, 404n14.

for English lay audiences. Moreover, translation projects, no less central to early English literary culture for conveying material that was not always originally English, brought devotional and philosophical ideas to broader audiences of learned people. But even these texts were of use to clerical as well as lay audiences. Such translations represented complex and innovative instances of reading and adapting classical learning, far beyond simply repackaging Latin texts in English terms, incorporating gloss traditions and revealing tantalizing details about the manuscript histories of the texts available to the early English.

4 Plain and Standard Styles

While the alliterative prose forms of Ælfric gets the lion's share of attention, not all early English prose was so overtly stylized, nor was style mutually exclusive with simplicity. The forms of individual *Chronicle* narratives, the Old English Benedictine office, or sermons like the Blickling homilies are less often considered for their forms, yet there are reasons to consider their structural and stylistic elements more extensively. So-called "plain style" was itself a deliberate formal choice and in some respects a formal innovation. It was also a rhetorical framing, a way that authors might explicate their own styles through an ideal that suggested who a text might be for and what purpose it might serve, particularly in devotional prose with particular claims to expressing truth. Alongside the more esoteric prose styles discussed in the previous section, we also see an apparently "standard" Old English prose form arise. But plain style was not only a concern relegated to vernacular writing, although a community's relationship to the vernacular inevitably played a role in what might be considered either standard or plain language. In Latin, too, early English writers complement the dense syntax and arcane vocabulary of hermeneutic Latin with straightforward, accessible Latin, responsive to the needs of both lay and clerical audiences, both at home and abroad. The present section considers early English efforts at plain or straightforward language, and the ways these things were deployed, as well as the existence and proliferation of the so-called "Standard Old English." These disparate focal points ask us to consider the ways that simple and standard language meant very different things in different social contexts, and offered different cues to different readers. These apparently unmarked forms demand scholarly attention no less than more overtly stylized language, and have as much to tell us about the working of forms in early English literature. The need for such styles invites further inquiry into the ways that form and function inhere in one another, but also pose difficulties to modern scholars in discerning what an apparently simple style might imply about those who used it or those by and for whom it was used.

The implications of a plain style are somewhat obscured from modern scholars by the rhetorical framing that authors often used in introducing it. While homilies or glosses often deploy a straightforward style with little comment, often discussions of plain style in early medieval writing work to position these texts against others in more elaborate styles, or to position the audiences that ostensibly need such plain language against those who do not. Some of this rhetoric has to do with concerns about the use of sacred and vernacular languages, which, as Nicholas Watson observes, differ in England from some of the concerns of writers on the continent. Medieval English was, of course, not mutually intelligible with Latin, unlike Romance languages such as French or Italian. For Francophone writers, then, distinguishing Latin, and keeping it distinct, from the vernacular was in practice a question of retaining the forms of sacred language as opposed to colloquial language, but crucially not a question of access – Latin remained intelligible if archaic to the laity who might hear it read.[130] For English-speaking writers and audiences, however, use of the vernacular was not merely a matter of slipping into more current or mundane spoken forms, but indeed a matter of who would be able to understand religious content at all. These linguistic dynamics shape the rhetorical framing of English-language texts as being ostensibly written for lower-status persons, such as parish priests and the laity, even when in practice those readers might have had functional Latin and higher-status ecclesiastical figures clearly used the English versions of texts, too.

"Plain" or standard style cuts across the boundaries of the types of forms we have considered so far. "Standard Old English" was the term Helmut Gneuss used to characterize the curious fact of the predominance of texts in the West Saxon dialect across Old English texts before the end of the tenth century, including in manuscripts written and read as far afield as Northumbria.[131] As Gneuss observes, "texts which had originally been written in Anglian were transcribed into late West Saxon, as was a large part of Old English poetry"; this standard linguistic practice forms a "standard literary language," a textual form that "extended its domain beyond the borders of this [West Saxon] dialect."[132] Subsequent research has upheld a remarkable consistency in the spelling of this "standard" Old English, across dialectal regions.[133] Often conflated with, but distinct from, this dialectal standardization is the more particular standardizing

---

[130] Watson, *Balaam's Ass*, I, 125–26.
[131] Gneuss, "The Origin of Standard Old English," 63–65.
[132] Gneuss, "The Origin of Standard Old English," 63.
[133] Faulkner, "Quantifying the Consistency of 'Standard' Old English Spelling."

of vocabulary during the Benedictine Reforms. Specifically emanating from Winchester and known as the "Winchester vocabulary," the Benedictine Reformers developed their own standard English vocabulary for ecclesiastical concepts and equivalents for Latin terms.[134] These apparent projects of standardization reflect centers of cultural influence, but differing motives for that influence. While much about standard Old English remains unclear, it comes to dominate "literary" language in the era from which the greatest number of extant Old English manuscripts, including all four of the major poetic codices, survive. It suggests the cultural associations and regional influences that shaped what literary texts were expected to look like. By contrast, the Winchester vocabulary had an initially more particular function and more limited scope, in standardizing vocabulary primarily for liturgical and institutional concepts, and especially vocabulary for Latin terms that might otherwise not have found a single precise vernacular equivalent.[135] While these versions of the vernacular may have been standardized, however, they remain distinct yet again from, although are sometimes related to, discussions of "plain" or "simple" language, or the designation of the vernacular as plain or simple by default. As we will see, neither standard nor plain language was ever truly simple.

For example, the idea of a "plain," or plainer, style was intermittently a justification for the writing of *opera geminata*, or at least for their prose halves. While Sedulius and Aldhelm argued for an aesthetic of completeness in composing "deliberately convoluted," complex prose, Bede "emphasises instead a criterion of general utility, based upon the familiar accessibility of prose, and entailing clarity of style."[136] Put another way, while some writers presented both the prose and verse halves of the *opus geminatum* as serving an aesthetic function in different styles, Bede's prose life of Cuthbert offers a functional, accessible complement to the dense and highly stylized verse, itself a complement to the earlier anonymous prose life. In prefacing his later prose life, Bede explains that he first scrutinized the life he had already written for the "certum cognitae veritatis indicium" (certain discovery of the known truth).[137] Incorporating names of sources and other details, then, Bede's prose life becomes both more accessible and ostensibly more verifiable, taking on what Godman calls a "quasi-historical manner."[138] Such clarity of style offers its own kind of beauty, and also offers another kind of truth – one foregrounding the presentation of facts as well as an economy of style. He dedicates the work to Bishop Eadfrith and the brothers at Lindisfarne, attributing even the

---

[134] Gretsch, "Winchester Vocabulary."   [135] Gretsch, "Winchester Vocabulary," 43–46.
[136] Godman, "The Anglo-Latin *opus geminatum*," 222.
[137] Colgrave, ed. and trans., *Two Lives of Saint Cuthbert*, 142.
[138] Godman, "The Anglo-Latin *opus geminatum*," 223.

liberty of having included a preface to the request of the brethren and the custom of including prefaces with works such as this one: "praefationem aliquam in fronte iuxta morem praefigerem" (that I should place in front some kind of preface, according to custom).[139] Moreover, Bede explains the process of showing his work to the priest Herefrith as he composed, revising as necessary, to the extent that he could "sicque ablatis omnibus scrupulorum ambagibus ad purum, certam ueritatis indaginem simplicibus explicatam sermonibus commendare menbranulis" (and thus having entirely removed everything of subtlety or ambiguity, set down to parchment the certain investigation of the truth explained in simple words).[140] Bede continues in a humble vein, describing the process of submitting the work to further authorities and suggesting the brethren at Lindisfarne themselves had brought further episodes to his attention that he had not been able to include in the completed work.

The preface, then, performs several kinds of work at once. For one, it valorizes its own simple and straightforward style, acknowledging the very different style of the preexisting version composed in what he calls "heroic verse" (*heroicis uersibus*).[141] Foregrounding the careful historical investigation that has preceded the current prose version, its self-professed simplicity of style bolsters its case for being a representation of carefully assembled factual information, free from embellishment and thus subject to and able to withstand further scrutiny and perusal by as many as possible. But in this it also foregrounds Bede's humility and obedience in producing an account for use of those who have requested it from him, whose prayers he seeks at the end of the preface. And Bede even attributes the fact of the preface itself to custom and request, rather than to any desire for flourish on his own part. Yet behind this simplicity lies complexity, a negotiation of complicated hierarchies and the desire to compliment the brethren at Lindisfarne, for whom Cuthbert was one of their own venerable forebears. Bede's claim to a simplicity of style bolsters his claim to have presented a bare, factual account; all the wonders attributed to Cuthbert become, in this framing, mere historical reporting.

Bede's example was one of those available to Alcuin of York, writing a few decades later in the Carolingian court. Alcuin also negotiates a complex web of social, cultural, and linguistic dynamics, in a context where Latin was not so far from the vernacular as it was in England and thus not able to be used in the same way to signal the rarefied learning of the elite as in England. Rather, for Alcuin, the standardizing of Latin vocabulary and style became necessary for

---

[139] Colgrave, ed. and trans., *Two Lives of Saint Cuthbert*, 142.
[140] Colgrave, ed. and trans., *Two Lives of Saint Cuthbert*, 144.
[141] Colgrave, ed. and trans., *Two Lives of Saint Cuthbert*, 146.

maintaining the distinctive character of Latin at all, which in continental Europe was in danger of adopting the colloquial forms of the Romance languages that existed in proximity with it. For this reason, standardizing Latin assured both that it would remain readable for other Latinate Christians in other places and times and that it would remain accessible for all Christians who might have access to Christian Latin texts. Nevertheless, for Alcuin, different kinds of texts have different purposes – of his *opus geminatum* the *Vita Willibrordi*, he suggests that the prose part, "unum prosaico sermone" (the one in prosaic speech), might be read aloud in church, while the verse might be more fit for private study by one who already knew the basic outline of the story.[142] As Godman observes, "never before had the verse part of a double work referred so often or so systematically to the prose."[143] The importance of plain language, for Alcuin, helped to undergird more elaborate compositions with straightforward expressions of fact without which they could not so easily be understood. His work moreover suggests, at least in part, how different forms might be used – those more straightforward, "prosaic" texts read aloud fit for the teaching and edification of all, while more complex verse read privately only by those with access and understanding.

Bede, of course, tells the truth that such prefatory remarks as his are customary. Writers' humility in describing their own language also took part in a highly conventional rhetoric that ironically displayed their affinities with an educated literary tradition. Later in the early medieval English period, Ælfric writes another preface (in Latin), using a different set of customs to address his Catholic Homilies (themselves in Old English) to a different audience, "ob edificationem simplicium" (for the edification of the simple).[144] As Jonathan Wilcox observes, Ælfric "repeatedly emphasizes simplicity of style," denying that he has "any ability in the artificial style," although of course he does so according to literary conventions of humility topoi.[145] Often, Ælfric's writing makes a certain claim to simplicity as Bede had done, but to slightly different ends. His choice of language in his prefaces, whether Latin or English, or the nature of information that he includes or excludes from his translations, reflects a sensitive attention to the audience he addresses.[146] When writing in English, Ælfric carefully establishes his authority through his relationship to monastic figures like Æthelwold, and reminds readers of his Latinate sources.[147] In rhetorically framing his role as the heir to these authorities and the means of relaying them to the laity in prose, his apparently simple prose style lends the air

---

[142] Godman, "The Anglo-Latin *opus geminatum*," 223–24.
[143] Godman, "The Anglo-Latin *opus geminatum*," 226.
[144] Gittos, "The Audience for Old English Texts," 235.   [145] Wilcox, *Ælfric's Prefaces*, 60–61.
[146] Wilcox, *Ælfric's Prefaces*, 63–67.   [147] Wilcox, *Ælfric's Prefaces*, 69–70.

of simply reporting well-established facts, not unlike the approach taken by Bede in the preface to the prose life of Cuthbert. In the Latin preface to the *Catholic Homilies*, then, he explains that in order to educate the simple, "nec obscura posuimus verba, sed simplicem Anglicam, quo facilius possit ad cor pervenire legentium vel audientium ad utilitatem animarum suarum" (we do not set down obscure words, but simple English, which can more easily penetrate the heart of those either reading or hearing for the use of their souls).[148] While the English preface focuses on the correction of error that Ælfric hopes to accomplish through his writings, the Latin makes explicit the connection between the form of his words and their efficacy. Ælfric makes a similar move in the Latin preface to his *Grammar*:

> Scio multimodis verba posse interpretari, sed ego simplicem interpretationem sequor, fastidii vitandi causa. ... nos contenti sumus, sicut didicimus in scola Aðelwoldi venerabilis presulis, qui multos ad bonum imbuit.[149]
>
> I know words are able to be interpreted in various ways, but I follow the simple interpretation, for the sake of avoiding revulsion. ... We are content, following what we learned in the school of the venerable bishop Æthelwold, who imbued many people with good.

Acknowledging, briefly, the possibility of diverse interpretations, Ælfric declares not only that he has chosen the simple meaning but that he does so in mere humble accordance with his own teaching – teaching received in the school of one of the great monastic authorities of his time.

Helen Gittos has cautioned that early medieval English writers often frame vernacular texts as a concession, an aid for those unable to access or read Latin texts, regardless of the real difficulty or intended audience of that vernacular text in practice. This convention, as Gittos demonstrates, stretches from the lament for the state of Latin learning and justification for vernacular translation in the Alfredian *Pastoral Care*, to texts ostensibly addressed to the laity, novices, or secular clergy in the decades after the Benedictine Reforms.[150] But as she further demonstrates, we should not always believe the claims these texts make about themselves. Stephenson has also written about the dynamics of the use of English in and after the tenth-century Benedictine Reforms in particular: Byrhtferth of Ramsey, as we saw before, intersperses simple Old English passages among both Latin both simple and complex in his *Enchiridion*.[151] But Gittos shows that Old English texts often, when they make statements about either their authors or audiences, use conventions

---

[148] Wilcox, *Ælfric's Prefaces*, 107.   [149] Wilcox, *Ælfric's Prefaces*, 114–15.
[150] Gittos, "The Audience for Old English Texts," 235–36.
[151] Stephenson, *The Politics of Language*.

that should not be taken literally. Gittos questions, for example, "the statement that the Old English Benedictine Rule was intended to be read by King Edgar, who was probably an infant when it was written," or, to take another example, the fact that Ælfric's *Lives of Saints* addresses itself to lay patrons, but both celebrates monastic saints and was in use in the monastery of Bury St. Edmunds.[152] While apologies for English translations reinforce the status of Latin and those who use it, in practice English texts and translations often had rather larger audiences, and the laity for whom English texts were supposedly made were not always ignorant of Latin, either. Plain style, then, exists to some degree in theory as much as in practice, and its practical applications were far from simple.

Related to plain style's focus on the utility of language were efforts to standardize language, or at least certain parts of language, both to enhance its usefulness and to minimize misunderstanding or misinterpretation. In Latin, the English writer Alcuin, working in the Carolingian court, embodies this ideal, while later on the Benedictine Reformers attempt a standardization of vocabulary in the English vernacular, particularly in the institutions associated with the influential bishop Æthelwold of Winchester. Ælfric, a student of Æthelwold's, was also, as Mechthild Gretsch puts it, "a painstaking practitioner of Winchester usage."[153] Moreover, as Gretsch notes, Ælfric specifically describes his translation choices as "straightforward," linking his approach to that which he learned at Æthelwold's school – but this vocabulary constituted less of a fully standardized form of the language than a "'professional' liturgical terminology," such as the loan word *ymen* for hymns, formulated for particularly crucial concepts within a specific sphere of reference.[154] Standardized language need not be language that would be considered straightforward in every given context. Yet for the Winchester Reformers and their students, such regular vocabulary sought to achieve in turn a regularity of interpretation for those who read it. Both Alcuin's efforts and those of the Winchester school and its descendants shared certain principles, while also navigating very different linguistic, social, and practical contexts.

The Benedictine Reforms were concerned with teaching, and with standardizing both practice and understanding across the English church. While the effectiveness and longevity of the movement may have been less than the Reformers might have wished, the textual legacy they left behind demonstrates the scope of their ambition. For one, the Reformers moved the English church away from the Roman version of the psalter to the Gallican psalter, in line with

---

[152] Gittos, "The Audience for Old English Texts," 239–40.
[153] Gretsch, "Winchester Vocabulary and Standard Old English," 47.
[154] Gretsch, "Winchester Vocabulary and Standard Old English," 47–50.

continental practice.[155] The Reformers also translated numerous Latin works into a form of English with their standardized lexicon and accessible style, contrasting sharply with their simultaneous use of a dense hermeneutic Latin, as explored in the previous section.[156] Their standardized vocabulary worked not only to establish standard terminology for important concepts but also to introduce and reframe new concepts. For example, Arendse Lund has traced how starkly the term *cynescipe* (kingship or, more precisely, "royal dignity") remained within the Æthelwoldian milieu, appearing in all but one instance in texts related to his circles.[157] This language, although standardized and therefore in some sense simplified, need not have been so accessible to the laity or to the unlearned; rather, the Winchester style required a certain amount of education and access for its terms to be properly understood. Importantly, however, the standardized vocabulary of the Reformers shared at least one central goal with Alcuin's standardized Latin – being of use for teaching the laity, and of teaching those who taught them, properly and without ambiguity, both in the language's accessibility and in its resistance to haphazard linguistic change, imposing the structures of monastic authority upon the use of language itself.

Plain style differs from, say, prose or verse, or various types of meter, in that it is often less defined by intrinsically recognizable formal features than by prefatory or interjected remarks explaining its simplicity. What defined simplicity, straightforwardness, or plainness in one context was not necessarily the same as what might define those things in another context. The conventional assertion of simplicity itself comprises a formal feature of the texts that bear it, and brings with it a complex set of associations with texts that have gone before. The tradition of plain or standard style, as it manifested in different ways across the pre-Conquest period, also suggests the impossibility of accounting for form apart from its complex social, historical, and political contexts. Bede's avowal of his use of plain style in Latin prose dedicated to the monks at Lindisfarne implicates a different set of hierarchical and social concerns than does that of the Benedictines' simple English prose style, complemented as it was by an esoteric and highly sophisticated Latin style that reinforced the shared identity of those who could understand it. Of course, Bede, too, composed complex Latin verses, as he did in the verse counterpart to his prose life. In these instances, one of the surest formal markers of a plain style is a highly elaborate style against which it might be juxtaposed. But plain style in its plainest sense unites simple elegance and utility. In this it reaches across the languages and centuries of early English literature, and anticipates the continuing role that the English vernacular would

---

[155] Gretsch, "Roman Psalter." [156] Stephenson, *The Politics of Language*.
[157] Lund, "*Cynescipe*," 55, 58–66.

play in pastoral instruction across the Conquest. As we will see in the next section, although English would change rapidly – obviating ideas of a standard English for centuries – it would retain many of its distinctive forms even as it incorporated new ones, preserving the same early English forms whose loss it records.

5 Later Forms

The literature of early medieval England had never been never monolingual. Yet after the Norman Conquest in 1066, both the English language and its cultural status changed rapidly, and English literature changed with it. Vernacular literature carried on in English, although its social and cultural roles were violently altered, and Anglo-Norman French took its place as the vernacular of the elite. New texts continued to be written in Anglo-Latin, documenting the new historical and institutional realities of England after the Conquest. Besides the linguistic changes that would, in time, transform what we recognize as Old English into early Middle English, the influence of Francophone literature introduced new literary forms, meters, and conventions into England. The status of the English language diminished and continued to shift in the decades after the Norman Conquest, catalyzing changes to language and literature as it even more profoundly restricted the contexts in which English was written and read. As French and Latin had become the languages of the court and of the church, English retained practical importance, if not so much prestige, as the language essential for instructing the laity, and thus a language in which texts of all kinds continued to be copied and translated. Despite all these changes, there are literary forms that persist even across the ruptures of the Conquest – formulaic language, literary topoi, and archetypal narratives and figures that changed but did not disappear entirely as time went on. In the twelfth century and later, scholars at Worcester in particular had a hand in preserving and adapting older forms to a changing English literary landscape. Texts including the Peterborough Chronicle, the *First Worcester Fragment*, or the *Soul's Address to the Body* reveal how post-Conquest writers copied, adapted, and imaginatively reflected upon earlier English forms using both new language and new forms available to them – including rhymed verse – that simultaneously displaced and preserved those forms that had gone before. In the forms that persist, we discover new ways that a literature the English were ostensibly losing could continue to function in a changing world. Even new bodies of literature reveal links to an earlier English past, and suggest the directions of England's literary future.

Early medieval England has often been studied as discontinuous from the central or high Middle Ages, from the post-Conquest medieval world of Romance and mysticism that would in turn give way to the heyday of Chaucer as the "father" of English literature and all that would follow him. Part of the reason for this has to do with the difficulty of the early forms of the language, but much of the disconnect arises from a modern sense of the kinds of literature that matter for a literary tradition. Modern literature prioritizes originality, and elevates the figures of individual authors as rare geniuses who produce what has never been seen before. As Elaine Treharne has put it, "[t]he moment of *original* composition is privileged as the only moment of significance when, really, each manifestation of a text has a great deal to reveal about the creator's intentions, purpose, and rhetorical situation."[158] These values are modern ones, not medieval ones. And since "from about 1020 or so there is barely any 'original' writing in English at all until about 1170," the texts surviving from that period have been too readily dismissed.[159] Adaptation, however, had always been central to the early English literary tradition, and even more straightforward copies have much to tell us about the literary forms that continued to matter in vernacular contexts as England underwent the upheavals of first Cnut's conquest in 1016 and the permanent alterations of the Norman Conquest of 1066.

Although late copies of early texts themselves have proven invaluable for study – such as the twelfth-century manuscripts of the Old English translation of Boethius, otherwise attested in full only in a charred Cotton manuscript from the tenth century – less has been said about the function of those copies in the time that produced them. Yet as Susan Irvine has argued, these manuscripts and the way they "are compiled carries important implications for their use."[160] As English continued as a language of pastoral care for the laity, homiletic texts continued to be copied and used. But verse forms survived and adapted as well, and the forms of earlier English histories (both in English and in Latin) shaped those that would come to be written. Moreover, even as new Anglo-Norman literary forms took root for the first time, they coexisted with existing English-language forms in ways that have yet to be more fully explored.

Verse forms, for one, offer a site of continuity as well as change. As discussed in Section 1, scholars have at times posited a "revival" of alliterative meter in the fourteenth century, since it was assumed that Old English metrical tradition could not have directly survived into that late period. But subsequent work began to shed light on how unlikely it would have been for a meter with such

---

[158] Treharne, *Living through Conquest*, 5.   [159] Treharne, *Living through Conquest*, 5.
[160] Irvine, "Compilation and Use of Old English Manuscripts," 42.

similar structures to have been rediscovered so long after Old English poetry in its most recognizable forms had ceased to be written. Following the work of Nikolai Yakovlev, scholars have developed systems for English alliterative meter based not on stress alone, but on prosody with which stress and alliteration coincide.[161] While particular aspects of verse prosody shift, the story of English alliterative meter is not the story of a tradition lost and re-found, or of a system of alliterative stress reclaimed and reinvented, but a story about vernacular grammar: As English grammar changes, the rules of what constitutes a strong position in English alliterative meter shift with it, gradually, and in ways that can be traced from Old English to late Middle English, with only relatively short gaps of time in which no alliterative poetry survives.[162]

In the centuries after the Norman Conquest, Worcester became a particularly important center in which Old English texts continued to be copied and read, and continued to exert their influence on new literary productions. The famous "Tremulous Hand" of Worcester carried out much of his work in this vein, adapting the spelling of Old English texts as they were copied to make their now-archaic dialects more accessible to post-Conquest readers of English. One of the Tremulous Hand's copies, the twelfth-century poem known as the *First Worcester Fragment*, or *Sanctus Beda*, offers a particularly poignant example of this late verse, although scholars debate just how early or late the poem is.[163] In the form in which it survives to us, in a single copy, it appears in a late dialect as a poem reminiscent *of* Old English literature that also reminisces *upon* Old English literature:

> Sanctus Beda was iboren her on Breotene mid us,
> And he wisliche bec awende
> Þet þeo Englise leoden þurh weren ilerde.
> And he þeo cnoten unwreih, þe questiuns hoteþ,
> Þa derne diȝelnesse þe deorwurþe is.
> Ælfric abbod, þe we Alquin hoteþ,
> He was bocare, and the fif bec wende,
> Genesis, Exodus, Vtronomius, Numerus, Leuiticus,
> Þurh þeos weren ilærde ure leoden on Englisc.[164]

[Saint Bede was born here in Britain among us, and he wisely translated books, so that the English people were taught through them. And he undid the knots, what are called questions, the secret mystery that is worthy. Ælfric the abbot, whom we call Alcuin, he was a writer and translated the five books,

---

[161] Yakovlev, "The Development of Alliterative Meter."
[162] Yakovlev, "The Development of Alliterative Meters"; as well as Weiskott, *English Alliterative Verse*.
[163] Cannon, *Grounds of English Literature*, 36–37.
[164] Edited in Brehe, "Reassembling the *First Worcester Fragment*," 530, lines 1–9.

Genesis, Exodus, Deuteronomy, Numbers, Leviticus; through these were our people taught in English.]

There are several ways that the poem valorizes peoples and culture close to home – although temporally quite distant, Bede was born, as we are told, "mid us," among us, specifically in Britain. And part of what he did that accrues such honor was translating books, so that other English people could benefit from his learning. Ælfric, too, becomes valorized as a translator, and to him is credited the translation of the first five books of the Bible, again so that English people could be taught in the English tongue. And if Ælfric gets conflated with Alcuin in this late text,[165] those names are both only part of a much longer litany of great men introduced in the poem's subsequent lines: "Oswald of Wireceastre, / Egwin of Heoueshame, Ældelm of Malmesburi, / Swiþþun, Æþelwold, Aidan, Biern of Wincæstre" (Oswald of Worcester, Egwin of Evesham, Aldhelm of Malmesbury, Swithun, Æthelwold, Aidan, Birinus of Winchester) are only some of the illustrious names called out by the poem.[166] But their memorialization testifies to their loss:

> Nu is þeo leore forleten, and þet folc is forloren.
> Nu beoþ oþre leoden þeo læreþ ure folc,
> And feole of þen lorþeines losiæþ and þet folc forþ mid.[167]

[Now is their teaching forsaken, and that people is lost. Now there is another people who teaches our folk, and many of the teachers are damned and the folk with them.]

The great teachers named in the previous lines are more than simply deceased; their loss and the loss of their teaching represent nothing less than the loss of those whom they edified through their teaching. Those who teach in their place now are simply "oþre leoden" (another people) and the people are as condemned by their teaching as they were edified by that of the great teachers of the English. As Brehe points out, after praising those who translated the Bible into English, the poem incorporates a Latin quotation from the Bible, "because there is no contemporary English translation" available in the poem's present.[168] Although the poem's focus on the "Englise leoden" (English people) as opposed to this "oþre leoden" (other people) suggests the effects of Conquest, as Christopher Cannon has

---

[165] Brehe argues that "it is unlikely that [the poet] believed Ælfric to be the Carolingian scholar," and suggests that the epithet might have designated Ælfric as "translator of Alcuin" from contemporaries who shared the name Ælfric; see "Reassembling the *First Worcester Fragment*," 531.
[166] Brehe, "Reassembling the *First Worcester Fragment*," 530, lines 12–14.
[167] Brehe, "Reassembling the *First Worcester Fragment*," 530, lines 17–19.
[168] Brehe, "Reassembling the *First Worcester Fragment*," 536.

written, the *First Worcester Fragment* represents "a written form whose near-destruction has come to seem synonymous with 1066 but which pays no attention whatsoever to either this year or its consequences."[169] Cannon has suggested that the "cataclysm" of the poem may be that of the earlier Danish Conquest, and that the poem in fact "proceeds as if 1066 had not *yet* happened."[170] The Norman Conquest itself receives no mention, nor does the poem specify just who the others who now teach the English are – are they Normans, or simply not monastic teachers like most of the named English teachers in the earlier section? Or are they simply English teachers, monastic or otherwise, simply less accomplished or virtuous than those who went before?

Ironically, of course, the *First Worcester Fragment* attests to just what has survived in the forms of English verse. As it laments the loss of great figures of the past who have left only crumbling monuments, half-understood by the lesser mortals of the world as it remains now, it, of course, recalls the forms of Old English elegies that had always lamented a greater past amplified by nostalgia and longing.[171] An Old English poem like *The Ruin* also spends the bulk of its length admiring the edifices that it must remind us have left only vestiges behind. Although the *Fragment* as we have it "spends fewer than three lines (17–19) lamenting anything," Brehe has shown how the poem conforms to vernacular alliterative verse forms, with small departures only where the list of names requires alteration to the alliterative pattern or introduces verses structured by rhyme – indeed, "a form consistent with Laʒamon's verse form except for the five end-rhymed lines."[172] As we have seen, short rhyming sections had never been alien to English verse, and by the twelfth century had become germane to it. Beyond the form of the meter itself, the conventions and topoi of the verse also recall the earlier English tradition – a tradition that fairly revels in the ache of memory for greater heroic figures now lost to time, whose crumbling monuments hint at the greatness they had once bestowed upon their people.

In this, the *First Worcester Fragment* attests to "the continued vitality of English" as well as "twelfth- and thirteenth-century interests in the Anglo-Saxon past."[173] Rather than the *enta geweorc* (work of giants) looked upon by the protagonist of *The Wanderer*, however, the speaker of the *First Worcester Fragment* looks upon the works of giants like Bede and Æthelwold, and the thriving English Church in the time before the Normans.[174] It commemorates

---

[169] Cannon, *Grounds of English Literature*, 20–21.
[170] Cannon, *Grounds of English Literature*, 36.   [171] Trilling, *Aesthetics of Nostalgia*.
[172] Cannon, *Grounds of English Literature*, 39; Brehe, "Reassembling the *First Worcester Fragment*," 531.
[173] Smith, *Arts of Dying*, 46–50.
[174] *The Wanderer*, line 87a, from Krapp and Dobbie, eds., *Anglo-Saxon Poetic Records*, vol. III.

these ecclesiastical giants in the form of another Old English trope, that of the catalogue poem.[175] As Brehe observes, "it is not clear how the poem ends because of the damaged state of the manuscript."[176] Nevertheless, like the elegiac poems in Old English that came before it, *The First Worcester Fragment* approaches its conclusion by resting its only future hope in heaven: "This beoþ Godes word to worlde asende/ Þet we sceolen fæier feþ festen to Him" (This is God's word sent to the world, that we shall fasten fair faith upon him).[177] Whether or not *The First Worcester Fragment* is a poem *about* the Norman Conquest, its language everywhere reflects knowledge of 1066, and 1016, of both William and Cnut, and of the poetic tropes that came before them. As Cannon suggests, it is our literary history, rather than the literature itself, that "makes the loss it claims to find" in erasing early Middle English literature and the literature of England just after the Conquest.[178] If the English of the *First Worcester Fragment* was no longer the language of government and administration or even the dominant language of literature in the wake of the Conquest, it nevertheless survives, persevering in this very poem that laments its apparent loss.

While the copying of *Old* English verse in the post-Conquest period became an increasingly niche project before eventually fading away, literature in English continued anyway. Poetic topoi from the earliest vernacular literature remain into later vernacular texts, melded with those of other Christian literary traditions.[179] Such meetings of literary forms can be witnessed on the page of Oxford, Bodleian Library MS Bodley 343, the sole manuscript witness to the late Old English poem *The Grave*. Although *The Grave* lacks the opening lines explaining the premise of a soul visiting its body in the grave, it evinces so many of the features of the poetic soul and body tradition that it has been repeatedly recognized as such by both modern scholars *and* medieval readers. The poem describes the grave as a house that is doorless ("Dureleas is þet hus") and laments how none of the body's friends in life will visit it now that its worldly trappings are gone.[180] It follows the earlier Old English *Soul and Body* poems in detailing how "wurmes þe todeleð" (worms dismember you).[181] And a later, thirteenth-century hand has added lines in English, translated from a French soul and body dialogue, *Un Samedi par nuit*, lamenting how no one will now deign to stroke the hair of the rotting corpse – lines

---

[175] Howe, *Old English Catalogue Poems*.
[176] Brehe, "Reassembling the *First Worcester Fragment*," 521.
[177] Brehe, "Reassembling the *First Worcester Fragment*," 530–31, lines 22–23.
[178] Cannon, *Grounds of English Literature*, 42.   [179] Lorden, *Forms of Devotion*, 110–64.
[180] Jones, ed., *The Grave*, line 13.   [181] Jones, ed., *The Grave*, line 16.

that only make sense if *The Grave* could be recognized as a soul and body dialogue, too:

> For sone bið þin hæfet   faxes bireued;
> al bið ðes faxes   feirnes forsceden;
> næle hit nan mit fingres   feire stracien.[182]

[For your head is quickly bereft of hair, the fairness of your hair is totally gone, no one at all will fairly stroke it with fingers.]

In their French source, these lines in turn adapt a passage from the Latin *Royal Debate* of the twelfth century, another soul and body text written in post-Conquest England that attests to just how much literature had changed. Rather than the pre-Conquest vernacular tradition of the soul *monologue*, in which only the soul speaks to a body that can no longer speak, nor yet apprehend the soul's speech as it awaits its resurrection and Final Judgment, the *Royal Debate* embodies a post-Conquest shift to soul and body *debates*, in which both sides speak.[183] Yet the *Royal Debate* even seems to play with the expectation of the body's failure to reply, as the soul remarks upon the body's inability to reply before the body suddenly sits up and begins to talk back.[184] But even across this substantial structural change, the remaining vernacular conventions of the soul and body topos remain strong enough in *The Grave* that this later reader could recognize them regardless, and extend them with the conventions of the later tradition.

With this history in view, then, a later poem like *The Soul's Address* carries on the traditions embodied in a late Old English poem like *The Grave*. Earlier English literary topoi of worldly transience, distinctive, though not exclusive, to the English tradition, carry on into poems like *Latemest Day*. In the same manuscript as the *First Worcester Fragment*, the poem known as *The Soul's Address to the Body* carries on and elaborates upon a specifically vernacular English poetic tradition. Soul and body debates are common enough throughout Christian literature, but, as mentioned earlier, the particular conceit of the soul's monologue, in which the decaying body cannot speak, predominates distinctively through the English tradition in the period before the Conquest.[185] The poem shares a number of features with the earlier Old English *Soul and Body* poems – primarily, the conceit of a distressed soul returning to its body in the grave sometime after death, but before their permanent reunion at the Final Judgment. As the only poem copied entirely by the scribe and glossator known as the Tremulous Hand, the twelfth-century *Soul's Address* alters Old English

---

[182] Jones, ed., *The Grave*, lines 23–25.   [183] Brent, "From Address to Debate," 3–14.
[184] Heningham, "Early Latin Debate," 166; see discussion in Lorden, *Forms of Devotion*, 115.
[185] Lorden, *Forms of Devotion*, 110–41.

prefixes to render its forms more readable to an audience already more familiar with the linguistic forms of early Middle English. But written in alliterating long lines, and evincing other tropes of earlier English verse, the poem embodies a continuation of early English literary forms even as it attests to how much the language has changed. The soul echoes that of its predecessor in Old English poetry in suggesting that it would have been better for both of them had the body never been born or received baptism than that it should earn the condemnation that it has. Like its Old English predecessor, the soul fixates upon the worms that gnaw the body in the grave, and the uselessness of the wealth and fine things it had accumulated for itself in life. At the same time, the soul of the *Soul's Address* appears as more overtly feminized than its Old English predecessors, going so far as to lament the offspring that it should have shared with its body – the spiritual fruition that the body neglected during its worldly life:

> Unker team is forloren   þe wit scolden teman
> so ic was þe bitæiht   þet wit scolden teman;
> þu scoldest beon bearne fæder   and ic hore moder;
> wit scolden fostrien bearn   and bringen ham to criste.[186]
>
> [Our offspring are lost, that we two should have brought forth, as I was given to you, that we two should have brought forth, and you should have been the father to, offspring, and I their mother, we two should have reared offspring, and brought them to Christ.]

As the vernacular tradition of the soul's monologue shifts across the Conquest, the more subtle feminization of the soul and its adoption of the trope of the woman's lament shifts, too, taking on more overtly romantic elements.[187] Given the starkly formulaic character of Old English poetry, such innovations may seem all the more alien to scholars of the tradition. Yet recombination of forms, even formulaic ones, had already been an integral part of the working of early English verse – now, however, previously remote forms of poetry and narrative become available to the tradition for the first time.

But verse hardly offers the only site where early vernacular English literary forms continued to exert influence into the later period. The bulk of Bodley 343, the same manuscript into which *The Grave* was inscribed, preserves homilies by Ælfric and Wulfstan, largely unchanged from their Old English versions, as well as anonymous Old English homilies and a bit of Augustine.[188] As Susan Rosser observes, the compiler of the collection selects largely "first-grade saints venerated by monks and laity alike," and homilies "mostly taken from the *Catholic*

---

[186] Moffat, ed., *Soul's Address*, Fragment G, lines 51–54.
[187] On the woman's lament trope, see Lorden, *Forms of Devotion*, 141–52.
[188] Ker, *Catalogue*, no. 368.

Homilies."[189] Although relatively few manuscripts from the twelfth century contain vernacular saints' lives, the evidence offers tantalizing clues to what has been lost, and frameworks for understanding the communities that still required texts like these saints' *vitae* and venerated the saints they spoke of.[190] Moreover, Anglo-Latin saints' lives played a crucial role in the decades after the Norman Conquest, "as a number of Latin *vitae* were rewritten by Norman writers for various reasons. Principally, the remodelling of *vitae* functioned in the appropriation of major English cults, placing a Norman stamp on the cult infrastructures already in place."[191] In this way, English hagiography carried on – but in Latin, rather than in English. William of Malmesbury's Latin translation of Coleman's life of Wulfstan offers one tantalizing example of this – although the Latin life allowed a crucial piece of English literary and religious culture to live on, the literary form of the text as it would have existed in its original language did not survive intact.

Early English historical sources provided the groundwork for post-Conquest histories to be written. As Anglo-Norman writers began to explain anew the place of England in a changing world, historical texts continued both to chronicle recent events and to retell and reframe the more distant past, drawing upon existing texts and forms in order to do so. Just as in the pre-Conquest period, however, literary forms routinely crossed boundaries of genre and language, and English language forms found their way into post-Conquest Latin as French forms found their way into English. Later poems included in versions of the *Anglo-Saxon Chronicle*, including poems on William the Conqueror, demonstrated in their very forms the incursion that the Normans represented – they include rhyme, and stray from the alliterative meter that had been the only vernacular meter in England before the Conquest.[192] The Anglo-Norman Henry of Huntingdon's twelfth-century *Historia Anglorum*, or "History of the English," evinces many of these phenomena simultaneously, adapting and combining English historical sources including Bede's *Historia ecclesiastica* and the *Anglo-Saxon Chronicle* along with works of church fathers like Jerome and Gregory the Great, as well as French sources and others now lost to us. In adapting material from the *Chronicle*, in particular, we can see how Old English vernacular forms transformed in the new context of a Latin historical chronicle. Henry even translates Old English poetry into Latin in his version of *The Battle of Brunanburh*, preserving elements of vernacular alliterative meter into Latin verse.[193] Just as his work embodies the profound changes

---

[189] Rosser, "The *Life of Martin* in Bodley 343," 135.
[190] Proud, "Extant Manuscripts," 117–120.   [191] Proud, "Extant Manuscripts," 119–20.
[192] Trilling, *Aesthetics of Nostalgia*; O'Brien O'Keeffe, "Deaths and Transformations."
[193] Weiskott, *English Alliterative Verse*, 183–86.

wrought by conquest, it also embodies vestiges of earlier English literary forms as well as the matter of earlier English literature that had lived through those forms.

Literature in England came to witness new forms, continuous only with literary forms imported from beyond English shores. In the century after the Conquest, while Worcester monks were still continuing to copy Old English homilies and poems, Marie de France composed *lais*, ostensibly translated from Breton into Anglo-Norman French, dedicated to the French-born king of England, Henry II. The *lais* are understood, rightly, as part of what would shape English literature to come – poems in this genre would be written in England throughout the following two centuries, from *Sir Orfeo* to Chaucer's *Franklin's Tale*. Yet they exist simultaneously, in the first century after the Conquest, with texts like *The Grave*, and with the tradition that would lead to the echoes of Old English in the thirteenth-century copy of the *Soul's Address to the Body*.

Scholars continue to debate just how the events of 1066 unfolded and reshaped the institutions and the cultural forms of medieval England. Cannon evocatively describes the interruption of the *Abingdon Chronicle* in the entry for this year, which breaks off, resumes, and breaks off again in the midst of the description of the Battle of Stamford Bridge: "here, the effects of the Norman Conquest are so severe that they preclude their own recording."[194] In the English language, original vernacular texts become sparse, as Treharne observes. Although, as Cannon writes, "Even in the twelfth century most of the survivals in English that we have been willing to call literature are fragments, snippets of poetry which sneak into texts in other languages," the question of what we call literature makes some difference, as does the fact that English existed within "the rich set of relations its production maintained with writing in Latin and Anglo-Norman."[195] Old English poetry, for its own part, survives in just four major manuscripts, most of which also contain prose homilies or saints lives, to which may be added, arguably, a fifth manuscript in the numerous poems of Cambridge, Corpus Christi College MS 201, as well as perhaps a sixth in the substantial collection of meters that intersperse the prose sections of the Old English *Boethius*. Literary texts in prose might include homilies, or the philosophical texts of the *Boethius* or the *Soliloquies*, or the adventures of *Apollonius*, but most of these texts were not original compositions in the vernacular. And as we have seen, even these sparse early literary texts retained a role and a familiarity among the textual culture that followed the

---

[194] Cannon, *Grounds of English Literature*, 17.
[195] Cannon, *Grounds of English Literature*, 19–20.

Conquest. But 1066 has had another role in established histories, as a demarcation of the end of one period and the beginning of another, in an act of periodization that Mary Rambaran-Olm has observed has misleadingly compelled us "to view time in a clear, teleological line rather than as a disorienting labyrinth."[196] Entirely apart from the consequences of Hastings, cultural history furnishes a narrative of a "high" Middle Ages that must emerge from the shadows of the "dark" ages by one means or another; the cessation of the cultural products of the earlier age taken as a given consequence of the slow progress toward the cultural products that remind modern scholars most of themselves.

Cultural change does not, however, proceed quite so neatly. Of course, the centuries after the Norman Conquest witnessed tremendous change to literary forms, as they witnessed changes to language, institutions, social hierarchies, and nearly everything else. But as readers in England lived through this change, they continued to recognize literary forms across it, and in many cases sought to preserve some sort of access to what had gone before. Indeed, the forms of earlier English literature could furnish these readers with the means to memorialize what they also preserved. Modern scholars may miss these correspondences across centuries when we read less widely than the medieval people we study did – or when our reliance on retroactive formal categories predetermines what we look for in the texts themselves. Literary form in early medieval England did not really come to an end even when other things did. Rather, the always protean forms of early literature in England continued to combine and shift as they encountered other forms of writing.

Afterword: What Is Form For?

Throughout this Element, I have considered the ways that literary form operated in the earliest centuries of English literature. In the end, these considerations return us to critical questions implicit from the outset. However much we might glean of early medieval forms through the evidence we have of their functions, the question remains: what is the study of form itself for, particularly regarding forms so remote from those of the present day? In some ways, highly conventional early medieval English literature has seemed less formally sophisticated than merely formulaic. But by expanding this question beyond the forms that have dominated critical attention, we can begin to see not only the formal variety of the earliest English literature but how those forms and their cultural functions connect to the periods and places early English literature influenced and was influenced by.

---

[196] Rambaran-Olm, "On or About 1066," 161.

The designation "formulaic" would likely not have seemed as pejorative to medieval writers and readers as it does to modern ones. Although modern literatures, too – from song lyrics to television shows to novels – rely on conventional forms and tropes to signal how audiences should understand them, modern readers and viewers tend to value how artists depart from those tropes in original ways, how they break with rather than how they use what came before. But if medieval readers were less concerned about originality and less put off by a bit of repetition, they also made forms anew – recombining them with other forms in new ways, or using them in surprising new contexts. Literary forms reveal cultural dynamics, however localized they may seem, that their broader historical contexts can never entirely explain. Old English riddles adapted from Latin incorporate the forms of elegiac monologues, for instance, and Anglo-Latin poetic half lines might take on the rhythms of vernacular verse. Devotional poems appropriate the topoi of heroic poetry, in ways more and less overtly critical of the ethos of worldly heroism. These formal innovations show, however, just how much was expected to be recognized from other contexts. Allusiveness often structured and enabled the elliptical forms of literary works that assume knowledge of what they say only succinctly or not at all. Forms, then, can reveal shared understandings and cultural histories by what they include as well as what they omit.

Modern readers can learn, too, from the scarce comments early writers made about their forms, in prologues to *opera geminata*, in glosses to copied texts, in the interjected commentary that writers sometimes offer in the midst of a narrative saint's life, or in remarks made in apology for a translation. But these comments, too, take part in conventional forms, topoi that we should not necessarily take at face value to understand their deeper connotations. Bede's apology for his translation of Cædmon's *Hymn*, for example, echoes a conventional distinction first made by Jerome on translating the Scriptures, but in doing so, Bede subtly suggests that the miraculous poem, composed spontaneously with divine assistance, is a holy text of another kind.[197] When the Old English *Boethius* preface uses a version of the trope, too, it asserts its place in an established and revered tradition of translation. The prologue of *Beowulf* does not only locate the poem's action in the long ago and far away, but invokes the shared stock of poetic formulas and topoi in which a prologue like this suggests what might be expected from stories like these. When the poem *Andreas* uses a version of this prologue in turn, it invites those heroic associations to both intermingle and contrast with the conventional tropes of the saint's life. And when an author asserts humility of one

---

[197] Bede, *Bede's Ecclesiastical History of the English People*, book iv, cap. 24.

kind or another, they also by that very conventional trope assert their own continuity with a grand tradition of texts that do the same.

This Element has sought to reframe the varied forms of early English literature, placing the more-studied forms of vernacular verse alongside less-studied Old English prose and Latinate forms to establish some measure of the formal variety of this time period. We began with verse, the sort of text where marked forms become most obvious. Yet while verse forms have received disproportionate attention relative to the amount of verse we have in the literature of the period, basic aspects of verse forms and conventions are nonetheless still hotly debated or only partly understood. The influence of continental Latin as well as Old Norse show their influence here, as in the rest of early medieval English literature, in ways only partially understood by modern scholars. Moreover, verse forms often mingled with various kinds of prose forms, or verse texts took prose texts as counterparts. Often translated in turn from Latin sources from outside of England, such texts are often studied within the framing of vernacular literary histories more readily defined – the so-called Alfredian translation program, or the major vernacular collections of homilies and saints' lives. Here, too, the categories within which we have studied and prioritized and anthologized early English texts have at times obscured the forms of the manuscripts that were once inseparable from the experience of the textual forms within them. We might think of how prose homilies and verse texts in the Vercelli book, for example, echo one another across differences in form and across different texts. And prose itself, often thought of as unmarked language, more of interest for the content that it conveys or the social and historical contexts that produce it and which it may reflect, also evinces crucial formal structures, including conventional structures, through which texts spoke to their original audiences and signaled how their authors wanted audiences to read them. But while the prose forms that share the most with verse – Ælfric's alliterating prose, for example – call the most attention to their forms, early English writers also took an interest in, and at times took pains to explain, "plain style" forms that appeared as stripped down as possible. Structuring and framing devices, designed to guide interpretation as well as to signal membership in – or exclusion from – textual communities become important in these texts, as do attempts to standardize speech. Finally, we have considered the ways that forms shift, but also persist, as the end of the early medieval period in England gives way to the high Middle Ages.

The forms I have discussed can call into question the received notions of literary history that pervade not only popular ideas of the "dark ages," but the priorities of literary scholarship on the period as well. Early literary and linguistic study shaped the structure and priorities of modern language departments in the academy, and offered broader scholarly foundations of study for many of the texts that are still most often edited, anthologized, and studied in the present century. The topography of this field in turn reinforces distinctions between bodies of texts based on periodization, or based on modern notions of what may be considered literary writing or not. As so many texts embody forms yet to be fully explored, and so many questions have yet to be asked of them, much of the story of English literary form remains inevitably as yet untold – we cannot yet know entirely what early English forms were for, or what stories they may yet have to tell.

Bibliography

Primary Sources

Aldhelm. *Aldhelmi Opera Omnia*, ed. R. Ehwald. Monumenta Germaniae Historica. Auctores Antiquissimi XV. Berlin: Weidmann, 1919.

Aldhelm. *Aldhelm: The Prose Works*, trans. Michael Lapidge and Michael Herren. Woodbridge: D. S. Brewer, 1979.

Bede. *Libri II de Arte Metrica et de Schematibus et Tropis*, ed. and trans. Calvin B. Kendall. Saarbrücken: AQ-Verlag, 1991.

Bede's Ecclesiastical History of the English People, ed. Bertram Colgrave and R. A. B. Mynors. Oxford: Clarendon Press, 1969.

Venerabilis Bedæ Anglosaxonis Presbyteri Opera Omnia, ed. J. P. Migne, vol. 5. Patrologiæ Cursus Completus Series Latina 94. Paris, 1850.

Byrhtferth of Ramsey. *Byrhtferth's Enchiridion*, ed. Peter S. Baker and Michael Lapidge. EETS s.s. 15. Oxford: Oxford University Press, 1995.

Campbell, A., ed. *The Chronicle of Æthelweard*. London: Thomas Nelson, 1962.

Colgrave, Bertram, ed. and trans. *Two Lives of Saint Cuthbert: A Life by an Anonymous Monk of Lindisfarne and Bede's Prose Life*. New York: Greenwood, 1969.

Dendle, Peter, ed. and trans. "The Old English 'Life of Malchus' and Two Vernacular Tales from the *Vitas Patrum* in MS Cotton Otho C.i: A Translation (Parts 1 & 2)." *English Studies* 90, nos. 5–6 (2009): 505–17, 631–52.

Dickins, Bruce, and R. M. Wilson, eds. *Early Middle English Texts*. New York: Norton, 1951.

Fulk, R. D., ed. *The* Beowulf *Manuscript*. Dumbarton Oaks Medieval Library. Cambridge, MA: Harvard University Press, 2010.

Fulk, R. D., Robert E. Bjork, and John D. Niles, eds. *Klaeber's* Beowulf, *Fourth Edition*. Toronto: University of Toronto Press, 2008.

Godden, Malcolm, and Susan Irvine, eds. *The Old English* Boethius: An Edition of the Old English Versions of Boethius's *De Consolatione Philosophiae*. 2 vols. Oxford: Oxford University Press, 2009.

Huemer, Johann. *Sedulius Opera Omnia*. CSEL 10. Vienna, 1885.

Irvine, Susan, ed. *The Anglo-Saxon Chronicle: 7. MS E*. Cambridge: Boydell & Brewer, 2004.

Jones, Christopher A., ed. *Old English Shorter Poems, Volume I: Religious and Didactic*. Cambridge: Harvard University Press, 2012.

Kramer, Johanna, Hugh Magennis, and Robin Norris, ed. and trans. *Anonymous Old English Lives of Saints*. Dumbarton Oaks Medieval Library. Cambridge, MA: Harvard University Press, 2020.

Krapp, George Phillip and Elliot Van Kirk Dobbie, eds. *The Anglo-Saxon Poetic Records*. 6 vols. New York: Columbia University Press, 1931–42.

Lapidge, Michael, ed. and trans. *Bede's Latin Poetry*. Oxford: Oxford University Press, 2019.

Lapidge, Michael, ed. and trans. *The Cult of St Swithun*. Oxford: Oxford University Press, 2003.

Lockett, Leslie. *Augustine's* Soliloquies *in Old English and in Latin*. Cambridge, MA: Harvard University Press, 2022.

Malone, Kemp, ed. *Deor*, rev. ed. Exeter: Exeter University Press, 1977.

Moffat, Douglas, ed. *The Soul's Address to the Body: The Worcester Fragments*. East Lansing, MI: Colleagues Press, 1987.

Scragg, Donald, ed. *The Vercelli Homilies and Related Texts*. EETS o.s. 300. Oxford: Oxford University Press, 1992.

Skeat, W. W., ed. *Ælfric's Lives of Saints*. EETS 76, 82, 94, 114. London: Oxford University Press, 1881–1900.

Sweet, Henry, ed. *King Alfred's West Saxon Version of Gregory's Pastoral Care*. EETS 45, 50. London, 1871.

Wilcox, Jonathan, ed. *Ælfric's Prefaces*. Durham: Durham Medieval Texts, 1994.

Secondary Sources

Beechy, Tiffany. *The Poetics of Old English*. Farnham: Ashgate, 2010.

Blair, John. *The Church in Anglo-Saxon Society*. Oxford: Oxford University Press, 2005.

Bredehoft, Thomas. *Early English Metre*, 2nd ed. Toronto: University of Toronto Press, 2005.

Brehe, S. K. "Reassembling the *First Worcester Fragment*." *Speculum* 65 (1990): 521–36.

Brent, J. Justin. "From Address to Debate: Generic Considerations in the Debate between Soul and Body." *Comitatus* 32 (2001): 1–18.

Brljak, Vladimir. "Unediting *Deor*." *Neuphilologische Mitteilungen* 112, no. 3 (2011): 297–321.

Bullough, D. A. "Reminiscence and Reality: Text, Translation and Testimony of an Alcuin Letter." *Journal of Medieval Latin* 5 (1995): 174–201.

Cannon, Christopher. *The Grounds of English Literature*. Oxford: Oxford University Press, 2004.

Carlson, David. "Africa and England *c.* 700: Aldhelm and P. Optatianus Porphyrius," *Nottingham Medieval Studies* 61 (2017): 9–37.

Claassen, Jo-Marie. "Literary *Anamnesis*: Boethius Remembers Ovid." *Helios* 34, no. 1 (2007): 1–35.

Clark, Amy W. "Familiar Distances: Beating the Bounds of Early English Identity." PhD Diss., University of California, Berkeley, 2020.

Clayton, Mary. "Homiliaries and Preaching in Anglo-Saxon England." In *Old English Prose: Basic Readings*, ed. Paul Szarmach, 151–98. New York: Garland, 2000.

Cornelius, Ian. *Reconstructing Alliterative Verse: The Pursuit of a Medieval Meter*. Cambridge: Cambridge University Press, 2017.

Cornelius, Ian, and Eric Weiskott. "The Intricacies of Counting to Four in Old English Poetry." *Language and Literature* 30, no. 3 (2021): 249–75.

Cubitt, Catherine. "Ælfric's Lay Patrons." In *A Companion to Ælfric*, ed. Hugh Magennis and Mary Swan, 165–92. Leiden: Brill, 2009.

Davis, Kathleen. *Periodization and Sovereignty: How Ideas of Feudalism and Secularization Govern the Politics of Time*. Philadelphia: University of Pennsylvania Press, 2008.

Donoghue, Daniel. *How the Anglo-Saxons Read Their Poems*. Philadelphia: University of Pennsylvania Press, 2018.

Dumitrescu, Irina. *The Experience of Education in Anglo-Saxon Literature*. Cambridge: Cambridge University Press, 2018.

Faulkner, Mark. "Quantifying the Consistency of 'Standard' Old English Spelling." *Transactions of the Philological Society* 118, no. 1 (2020): 192–205.

Fiedler, H. G. "The Sources of the First Blickling Homily." *Modern Language Quarterly* 6 (1903): 122–24.

Foley, John Miles. *Immanent Art: From Structure to Meaning in Traditional Oral Epic*. Bloomington: Indiana University Press, 1991.

"Texts that Speak to Readers Who Hear: Old English Poetry and the Language of Oral Tradition." In *Speaking Two Languages: Traditional Disciplines and Contemporary Theory in Medieval Studies*, ed. Allen Frantzen, 141–56. Albany, NY: SUNY Press, 1991.

Frank, Roberta. "The Search for the Anglo-Saxon Oral Poet," *Bulletin of the John Rylands University of Manchester*, 75, no. 1 (1993): 11–36.

"A Taste for Knottiness: Skaldic Art at Cnut's Court." *Anglo-Saxon England* 47 (2018): 197–217.

Friesen, Bill. "Visions and Revisions: The Sources and Analogues of the Old English *Andreas*." PhD Diss., University of Toronto, 2008.

Fry, Donald K. "Old English Formulaic Themes and Type-Scenes." *Neophilologus* 52, no. 1 (1968): 48–54.

Fulk, R. D. *A History of Old English Meter*. Philadelphia: University of Pennsylvania Press, 1992.

Gatch, Milton McC. "King Alfred's Version of Augustine's *Soliloquia*: Some Suggestions on Its Rationale and Unity." *Old English Prose: Basic Readings*, ed. Paul Szarmach, 199–236. New York: Garland, 2000.

Gittos, Helen. "The Audience for Old English Texts: Ælfric, Rhetoric, and 'the Edification of the Simple'." *Anglo-Saxon England* 43 (2014): 231–66.

Gneuss, Helmut. "The Origin of Standard Old English and Æthelwold's School at Winchester." *Anglo-Saxon England* 1 (1972): 63–83.

Godden, Malcolm. "Did King Alfred Write Anything?" *Medium Ævum* 76, no. 1 (2007): 1–23.

Godman, Peter. "The Anglo-Latin *opus geminatum*: From Aldhelm to Alcuin." *Medium Ævum* 50, no. 2 (1981): 215–29.

Gretsch, Mechthild. "The Roman Psalter, Its Old English Glosses and the English Benedictine Reform." In *The Liturgy of the Late Anglo-Saxon Church*, ed. Helen Gittos and M. Bradford Bedingfield, 13–28. Woodbridge: Boydell & Brewer, 2005.

"Winchester Vocabulary and Standard Old English: The Vernacular in Late Anglo-Saxon England." *Bulletin of the John Rylands Library* 83, no. 1 (2001): 41–87.

Hanna, Ralph. "Alliterative Poetry." In *The Cambridge History of Medieval English Literature*, ed. David Wallace, 488–512. Cambridge: Cambridge University Press, 1999.

Heningham, Eleanor K. "An Early Latin Debate of the Body and Soul Preserved in MS Royal 7 A III in the British Museum." PhD Diss., New York University, 1937.

Howe, Nicholas. *The Old English Catalogue Poems*. Copenhagen: Rosenkilde & Bagger, 1985.

Irvine, Susan. "The Compilation and Use of Manuscripts Containing Old English in the Twelfth Century." In *Rewriting Old English in the Twelfth Century*, ed. Mary Swan and Elain M. Treharne, 41–61. Cambridge: Cambridge University Press, 2000.

Ker, N. R. *Catalogue of Manuscripts Containing Anglo-Saxon*. Oxford: Clarendon Press, 1957.

Kim, Susan M. "'In his heart he believed in God, but he could not speak like a man': Martyrdom, Monstrosity, Speech, and the Dog-Headed Saint Christopher." In *Writers, Editors, and Exemplars in Medieval English Texts*, ed. S. M. Rowley, 235–50. London: Palgrave, 2021.

Lapidge, Michael. *Anglo-Latin Literature*, 2 vols. London: Hambledon Press, 2003–2004.

"The School of Theodore and Hadrian." *Anglo-Saxon England* 15 (1986): 45–72.

Lorden, Jennifer A. *Forms of Devotion in Early English Poetry: The Poetics of Feeling*. Cambridge: Cambridge University Press, 2023.

"Landscapes of Devotion: The Settings of St Swithun's Early *uitae*." *Anglo-Saxon England* 45 (2016): 285–309.

"Revisiting the Legendary History of *Deor*." *Medium Ævum* 90, no. 2 (2021): 197–216.

"Tale and Parable: Theorizing Fictions in the Old English *Boethius*." *PMLA* 136, no. 3 (2021): 340–55.

Lund, Arendse. "*Cynescipe*, Bishop Æthelwold, and the Spread of Legal Language." *Law, Literature, and Social Regulation in Early Medieval England*, ed. Anya Adair and Andrew Rabin, 54–67. Woodbridge: Boydell & Brewer, 2023.

Magoun, Francis P., Jr. "Oral-Formulaic Character of Anglo-Saxon Narrative Poetry." *Speculum* 28, no. 3 (1953): 446–67.

Morini, Carla. "The Old English *Apollonius* and Wulfstan of York." *Leeds Studies in English*, n.s. 36 (2005): 63–104.

Niles, John D. *The Idea of Anglo-Saxon England 1066–1901: Remembering, Forgetting, Deciphering, and Renewing the Past*. Oxford: Wiley, 2015.

O'Brien O'Keeffe, Katherine. "Deaths and Transformations: Thinking through the 'End' of Old English Verse." *New Directions in Oral Theory*, ed. Mark C. Amodio, 149–78. Tempe, AZ: ACMRS, 2005.

Visible Song: Transitional Literacy in Old English Verse. Cambridge: Cambridge University Press, 1990.

Orchard, Andy, ed. *The Old English and Anglo-Latin Riddle Tradition*. Dumbarton Oaks Medieval Library. Cambridge, MA: Harvard University Press, 2021.

Powell, Allison. "Verbal Parallels in *Andreas* and its Relationship to *Beowulf* and Cynewulf." PhD Diss., University of Cambridge, 2002.

Proud, Joanna. "Old English Prose Saints' Lives in the Twelfth Century: The Evidence of the Extant Manuscripts." *Rewriting Old English in the Twelfth Century*, ed. Mary Swan and Elain M. Treharne, 117–31. Cambridge: Cambridge University Press, 2000.

Rambaran-Olm, Mary. "On or About 1066." *The Routledge Companion to Politics and Literature in English*, ed. Matthew Stratton, 161–71. London: Routledge, 2023.

"A Wrinkle in Medieval Time: Ironing Out Issues of Race, Temporality, and the Early English." *New Literary History* 52, nos. 3–4 (2021): 385–406.

Reider, Alexandra. "*The Phoenix* and the Interlingual Dimensions of Early English Literary Culture." *JEGP* 121, no. 4 (2022): 431–51.

Reynolds, Susan. "What Do We Mean by 'Anglo-Saxon' and 'Anglo-Saxons'?" *Journal of British Studies* 24, no. 4 (1985): 395–414.

Rosser, Susan. "Old English Prose Saints' Lives in the Twelfth Century: The *Life of Martin* in Bodley 343." *Rewriting Old English in the Twelfth Century*, ed. Mary Swan and Elaine M. Treharne, 132–42. Cambridge: Cambridge University Press, 2000.

Sievers, Eduard. *Altgermanische Metrik*. Halle: Max Niemeyer, 1893.

Smith, D. Vance. *Arts of Dying: Literature and Finitude in Medieval England*. Chicago, IL: University of Chicago Press, 2020.

Smith, Scott Thompson. "The Edgar Poems and the Poetics of Failure in the *Anglo-Saxon Chronicle*." *Anglo-Saxon England* 39 (2010): 105–37.

Stanley, Eric. *The Search for Anglo-Saxon Paganism*. Cambridge: D. S. Brewer, 1964. Reprinted in *Imagining the Anglo-Saxon Past: The Search for Anglo-Saxon Paganism and Anglo-Saxon Trial by Jury*. Cambridge: D. S. Brewer, 2000.

―――. "Wulfstan and Ælfric: 'The True Difference between the Law and the Gospel.'" *Wulfstan, Archbishop of York: The Proceedings of the Second Alcuin Conference*, ed. Matthew Townend, 429–41. Turnhout, Brepols, 2004.

Stephenson, Rebecca. "Ælfric of Eynsham and Hermeneutic Latin: 'Meatim Sed et Rustica' Reconsidered." *Journal of Medieval Latin* 16 (2006): 111–41.

―――. *The Politics of Language: Byrhtferth, Ælfric, and the Multilingual Identity of the Benedictine Reform*. Toronto: University of Toronto Press, 2015.

Thomas, Daniel. "A Close Fitt: Reading *Beowulf* Fitt II with the *Andreas* Poet," *Anglo-Saxon England* 48 (2019): 1–41.

Thornbury, Emily. *Becoming a Poet in Anglo-Saxon England*. Cambridge: Cambridge University Press, 2014.

―――. "The Ornament of Virginity: Aldhelm's *De uirginitate* and the Virtuous Women of the Early English Church." In *Feminist Approaches to Early Medieval English Studies*, ed. Robin Norris, Rebecca Stephenson, and Renée R. Trilling, 171–95. Amsterdam: Amsterdam University Press, 2023.

Treharne, Elaine. "Categorization, Periodization: The Silence of (the) English in the Twelfth Century." *New Medieval Literatures* 8 (2006): 247–73.

―――. *Living through Conquest: The Politics of Early English, 1020–1220*. Oxford: Oxford University Press, 2012.

Trilling, Renée. *The Aesthetics of Nostalgia: Historical Representation in Old English Verse*. Toronto: University of Toronto Press, 2009.

Tyler, Elizabeth M. *Old English Poetics: The Aesthetics of the Familiar in Anglo-Saxon England*. York: York Medieval Press, 2006.

Watson, Nicholas. *Balaam's Ass, Volume I: Frameworks, Arguments, English to 1250*. Philadelphia: University of Pennsylvania Press, 2022.

Weaver, Erica. "Hybrid Forms: Translating Boethius in Anglo-Saxon England." *Anglo-Saxon England* 45 (2016): 213–38.

Weiskott, Eric. *English Alliterative Verse: Poetic Tradition and Literary History*. Cambridge: Cambridge University Press, 2016.

Weston, Lisa M. "Honeyed Words and Waxen Tablets: Aldhelm's Bees and the Materiality of Anglo-Saxon Literacy." *Mediaevalia* 41 (2020): 43–69.

Whatley, E. Gordon. "Lost in Translation: Omission of Episodes in Some Old English Prose Saints' Legends." *Anglo-Saxon England* 26 (1997): 187–208.

Whitelock, Dorothy, "The Prose of Alfred's Reign." In *Continuations and Beginnings: Studies in Old English Literature*, ed. Eric Stanley, 67–103. London: Nelson, 1966.

Wilton, David. "What Do We Mean by Anglo-Saxon? Pre-Conquest to the Present." *JEGP* 119, no. 4 (2020): 425–56.

Yakovlev, Nikolai. "The Development of Alliterative Metre from Old to Middle English." DPhil Thesis, University of Oxford, 2008.

Acknowledgments

I am grateful to the editors of this series, Megan Cavell, Rory Naismith, Winfried Rudolf, and particularly Emily Thornbury for inviting me to write this Element and for support along the way, and to my anonymous reviewers for helpful feedback. And I'm grateful to Amy W. Clark for everything, always.

Cambridge Elements

England in the Early Medieval World

Megan Cavell
University of Birmingham

Megan Cavell is Associate Professor in Medieval English Literature at the University of Birmingham. She works on a wide range of topics in medieval literary studies, from Old and early Middle English and Latin languages and literature to riddling, gender and animal studies. Her previous publications include *Weaving Words and Binding Bodies: The Poetics of Human Experience in Old English Literature* (2016), *Riddles at Work in the Early Medieval Tradition: Words, Ideas, Interactions* (co-edited with Jennifer Neville, 2020), and *The Medieval Bestiary in England: Texts and Translations of the Old and Middle English Physiologus* (2022).

Rory Naismith
University of Cambridge

Rory Naismith is Professor of Early Medieval English History in the Department of Anglo-Saxon, Norse and Celtic at the University of Cambridge, and a Fellow of Corpus Christi College, Cambridge. Also a Fellow of the Royal Historical Society, he is the author of *Early Medieval Britain 500–1000* (Cambridge University Press, 2021), *Citadel of the Saxons: The Rise of Early London* (2018), *Medieval European Coinage, with a Catalogue of the Coins in the Fitzwilliam Museum, Cambridge, 8: Britain and Ireland c. 400–1066* (Cambridge University Press, 2017) and *Money and Power in Anglo-Saxon England: The Southern English Kingdoms 757–865* (Cambridge University Press, 2012, which won the 2013 International Society of Anglo-Saxonists First Book Prize).

Winfried Rudolf
University of Göttingen

Winfried Rudolf is Chair of Medieval English Language and Literature in the University of Göttingen (Germany). Recent publications include *Childhood and Adolescence in Anglo-Saxon Literary Culture* (with Susan E. Irvine, 2018). He has published widely on homiletic literature in early England and is currently principal investigator of the ERC-Project ECHOE–Electronic Corpus of Anonymous Homilies in Old English.

Emily V. Thornbury
Yale University

Emily V. Thornbury is Associate Professor of English at Yale University. She studies the literature and art of early England, with a particular emphasis on English and Latin poetry. Her publications include *Becoming a Poet in Anglo-Saxon England* (Cambridge, 2014) and, co-edited with Rebecca Stephenson, *Latinity and Identity in Anglo-Saxon Literature* (University of Toronto Press, 2016). She is currently working on a monograph called *The Virtue of Ornament*, about pre-Conquest theories of aesthetic value.

About the Series

Elements in England in the Early Medieval World takes an innovative, interdisciplinary view of the culture, history, literature, archaeology and legacy of England between the fifth and eleventh centuries. Individual contributions question and situate key themes, and thereby bring new perspectives to the heritage of early medieval England. They draw on texts in Latin and Old English as well as material culture to paint a vivid picture of the period. Relevant not only to students and scholars working in medieval studies, these volumes explore the rich intellectual, methodological and comparative value that the dynamic researchers interested in England between the fifth and eleventh centuries have to offer in a modern, global context. The series is driven by a commitment to inclusive and critical scholarship, and to the view that early medieval studies have a part to play in many fields of academic research, as well as constituting a vibrant and self-contained area of research in its own right.

Cambridge Elements

England in the Early Medieval World

Elements in the Series

Crime and Punishment in Anglo-Saxon England
Andrew Rabin

Europe and the Anglo-Saxons
Francesca Tinti

Art and the Formation of Early Medieval England
Catherine E. Karkov

Writing the World in Early Medieval England
Nicole Guenther Discenza and Heide Estes

Multilingualism in Early Medieval Britain
Lindy Brady

Recovering Old English
Kees Dekker

Health and the Body in Early Medieval England
Caroline Batten

Entertainment, Pleasure, and Meaning in Early England
Martha Bayless

Visions of Hierarchy and Inequality in Early Medieval England
Stuart Pracy

Literary Form in Early Medieval England
Jennifer A. Lorden

A full series listing is available at: www.cambridge.org/EASW

For EU product safety concerns, contact us at Calle de José Abascal, 56–1°,
28003 Madrid, Spain or eugpsr@cambridge.org.

www.ingramcontent.com/pod-product-compliance
Lightning Source LLC
LaVergne TN
LVHW020351260326
834688LV00045B/1670